BE YOUR OWN
LIFE COACH

BE YOUR OWN LIFE COACH

HOW TO LIFE COACH YOURSELF INTO WHAT YOU WANT

DR. DIONNA HANCOCK-JOHNSON

Hancock-Johnsons Publishing Company™
P.O. Box 801961, Santa Clarita, CA 91380
www.hancockjohnsonpublishingcompany.com
Phone: 1-888-400-9766

© 2019 by Dionna Hancock-Johnson, EdD, MS, LSC All rights reserved.

No part of this book may be reproduced, stored in a retrieval system, or transmitted by any means without the written permission of the author.

Published by Hancock-Johnson Publishing Company 02/01/2019

ISBN: 978-0-9913988-3-6 (sc)
ISBN: 978-0-9913988-4-3 (hc)
ISBN: 978-0-9913988-5-0 (e)

Library of Congress Control Number: 2012918853

Any people depicted in stock imagery provided by Thinkstock are models, and such images are being used for illustrative purposes only.

Certain stock imagery © Thinkstock. This book is printed on acid-free paper.

Because of the dynamic nature of the Internet, any web addresses or links contained in this book may have changed since publication and may no longer be valid. The views expressed in this work are solely those of the author and do not necessarily reflect the views of the publisher, and the publisher hereby disclaims any responsibility for them.

Acknowledgements

Thank GOD first and foremost! This has been such a journey of deciding which book should be my debut! When my children's book was put on a year hold due to some drawing technicalities, it wasn't my intention to have this as my next piece of work but sometimes you have to move in a different direction when God asks you to. That was sure the case for this book! Four manuscripts later, I am very pleased to present this to you as my first self-help title. In reading this book, I hope that you can find something meaningful to help you grow on your path to success.

Thank you to everyone who believed in me and waited patiently for my first creations to be birthed. A special thank you goes to my family for allowing mommy to stay up and work when I should have been in bed with you all. Another huge thank you goes to my East Coast family who never gives up on me, friends and family around the world, and to those who pre-read, edited, and endorsed my book.

Author's Inspiration Notes

I originally wanted to write this book to give you a place where you can read some of my real-life experiences of how I got on the road to life coaching myself into who I am today. I wanted to write a book that could give you real life examples that you may relate to but never the less could get you thinking of how you can life coach yourself into the person you would like to be some day. In addition, I wanted to show you (my readers) some of the experiences I have struggled with on a day-to-day basis while I was becoming the person I wanted to be. I am not a writer that writes just because I know how or because of my degrees but I am a writer that writes because it is a gift that I cannot seem to keep to myself. They say when something is in God's plan, you have no say in how it will unfold; this has been true for me because of where I am today!

During the final process of writing this book, I gained a different vision for writing something more than just a manual to life coaching yourself into success, but also something that could allow you (my readers) to read life quotes from others around the world that are just as successful, in one book. I believe that if you could hear it not only from me, but also from other celebrities that you look up to, you could gain the inspiration and motivation you need to become successful at whatever it is your heart desires.

Finally, I wrote this book because there is a need to help others like me who sometimes struggle with getting what they want out of life. Just because I am successful now does not mean I did not have life circumstances that hindered my success, too.

Table Of Contents

Chapter	Page
Introduction	1
1 What Does Life Mean To You?	5
2 What Does Life Coaching Yourself Mean?	9
3 Do You Trust Yourself?	11
4 Know What Your Purpose Is In Life	15
5 Dare To Dream But Don't Strive For Another's Dream	19
6 Think Like A Leader To Become One	25
7 Understand Failing Is Only The Beginning	29
8 Check Out Your Competition	35
9 Utilize Your Resources	39
10 Understand Others' Purpose In Your Life	43
11 Determine Who Is On Your Team	47
12 You Can't Make It With Negative Peers	49
13 Build Positive Energy Around Yourself	51
14 Build Credibility With Others Along The Way	55
15 Prepare For Change Before It Comes	61
16 Let Go Of What You Can't Change	63
17 Plan Your Goals	69
18 Set Real Life Goals	75
19 Clear The Clutter And Visualize Your Goals	79
20 Act Today For A Better Tomorrow	83
Chapter Activities Worksheet	87
Final Thoughts	95
References	97
About The Author	103
About The Photographer, Cover Designer, And Editors	105
Current And Future Products	107

Introduction

When you want something in life you go after it regardless of the obstacles that put a wrench in your plans; you still push forward to make it happen. That is if it means that much to you. I have been through experiences in my life that meant that much to me and I did what it took to fulfill those wants and desires.

That is what life is about! Learning how to go after your dreams and continuing to succeed at a higher level at all costs. When you go after what you want in life, you learn that you are pushed to a higher level by default. Sometimes your will power to attain what you want will take you on a road you didn't know existed. For example, say you make the decision to attend a college and you settle on a specific degree, but later find that you are interested in something else. After spending four years in one program your financial aid is maxed out, so you don't have the room to change your degree program. Now you must figure out how to go after what it is you want (i.e., the second-degree program). Now you begin to jump through hoops by going in and out of financial aid looking for additional funding, having meetings with local bank representatives, calling back home asking for financial support and other options.

These are not things you typically would do in a financial bind and, in fact, none of these things are things you have done in the past when you were in this type of situation. But now, because you want this "thing" (the second degree) more than anything before, you find yourself having the desire to make it happen. So, you come to a place where you do what you must, to see that desire through. Sometimes this takes seeking assistance from someone who is skilled at helping others fulfill their desires. Often these experts are referred to as "life coaches" people who help clients discover what they are unsure about in themselves, as well as helping clients learn how to make better life decisions on their own.

A life coach is known to give great insight on how to overcome stumbling blocks in your current life. A stumbling block is a figure of speech meaning that there is something stopping you from accomplishing what you want out of life. A stumbling block can also refer to anything that interferes with your success. It can vary from not having enough financial resources to start your dream job, to being told you cannot do something that your heart currently beats for in life.

A life coach is also good for walking a client through a series of steps on how to gain success in their life. I know it, because as a life coach myself, I am guilty of it! I often help clients discover what their true passion is in life by accessing their inner resources. I also help clients discover what they didn't think was discoverable, and sometimes that is the same will power needed to fulfill their lifelong desires. Sometimes even that is not enough!

What I find with my clients is that they sometimes like to take everything I offer in a session home with them for the long haul. In addition, over half of my clients have asked me to create a manual of the coping mechanisms/life coaching techniques that I use in my day-to-day coaching business. So I have finally taken the time to give my clients what they have been asking for: a personal life-coaching manual that they can use in their day-to-day life.

This book is not just for those that want to life coach themselves or teach themselves about life on a day-to-day basis; it is also for those who want to learn simple tactics on how to overcome life challenges when they want to be mentally and physically successful. This book demonstrates how you can avoid negativity, think like a leader, understand why and how failing occurs, become resourceful, set real-life goals, stay focused on those goals, determine who is really on your team of success, learn how to trust yourself, let go of what you cannot change in your life, and learn how to strive for your own dream rather than someone else's. In addition, readers will learn how to visualize right away their ultimate goals, make plans to achieve them and begin acting on them today.

This book is also for those who want to make changes in their life but are not sure how to get to that final goal. I truly hope you can take away one thing from this life-coaching manual and apply it to some areas of your home life.

For as long as I can remember, I have always been accountable for everything I have done in my life. Although, there were a few people in my life that had made a huge impact on my decisions during my journey, I have still been the only person accountable for where I am today. The things that I have learned on my journey have allowed me to take my career to a new level and experience things that I never imagined. I have learned that when you believe in something, you have to fight for it no matter what obstacles get in the way of you achieving these goals. Through all my struggles, the one thing that stayed consistent was my faith in God and my belief in myself that I could move beyond my struggles. Growing up I became obsessed with learning and it was my addiction of choice to escape the harsher times in my life. I medicated myself by educating myself. I basically life coached myself to be who I am and what I stand for today.

So, with this book I hope that you can take what you've learned on your personal journey and in your life coaching sessions to a new level by applying the methods from this book to your professional life and learn how to maintain them on a long-term basis.

Chapter 1
What Does Life Mean To You?

In order to take any steps toward life coaching yourself, you have to know what life means. That means understanding what your own meaning of life is; it starts with defining the word life. To think of it in a different way, try to finish this sentence (Life means _____ to me, or when I do this I get _____ out of life). If you are not able to fill in the blanks to either of these statements then this chapter is for you. The first step in learning to put the right words in the blanks above begins with understanding the generic definition of the word life as it is currently defined and then defining life as it relates to you. For example, life is currently defined as "the general or universal condition of human existence" (Merriam-Webster, 2012). To understand what life means to you, one must know their existence, and more specifically why they exist.

If you can determine why you are here on this Earth and what your calling is, then you can come to some conclusion as to what life means to you.

When you know what life means to you, it can bring clarity to your world and to others around you. If you don't know what life means to you, then others around you will not know what life means for you either. Just think of those people you may have come across who seem like they have life all figured out. From the way they dress, to their mannerisms, to their way of speaking, they always appear to know what they want in life and how to go after it.

After this observation, you begin to wonder whether your own ducks are in order and if you are giving off the same appearance to them. Self-consciously you hope to have the same effect on others but you are not sure since you do not know what life means to you. From that moment, those thoughts begin to eat up at your inside until you know for sure. So, in a situation like this what do you do? You start calling everyone you know, asking them if your appearance speaks of confidence, boldness, and assurance, just as you witnessed with that person earlier. Irritated with not getting the answers you feel you deserve, you eventually flat out ask them if you come across to them as if you have life all figured out. When their response is "Yes," you begin to feel comfortable again with who you are, the decisions you have made in your life and the lessons you think you have learned about life. But when that friend's response is "No," you lose it! You continue to second-guess all the decisions you have made that put you in the situation you are in at that moment. To add insult to injury, the confidence you once boasted or that knowledge you once kicked to a family member or friend about having life all figured out, seems very far from the feelings you are experiencing now. So, now you are disappointed with yourself and your life.

The problem you have here is that you have to know what life means to you. Once you know what life means to you, you can begin to breathe life into your purpose. On the other hand, waiting 20 years to do something is only going to verify what you did not know, because you never took the time to learn what life meant to you.

Just think, if you would have had life figured out by now, you would know, and those around you would know it too. In fact they would be the first to testify to that. Friends and family members, who associate themselves with someone who is successful and appears to have it all together in their life, will tell the world.

However, if you are one of those people who appears on the surface to have life all figured out and most of the time seem lost at life's pace, then those around you would testify to that, too, but in a negative way. At this point, what are they thinking? Exactly, that you are a failure, you are confused, not sure where to go and what direction to walk in. They would just make fun of you instead of lifting you up; they would be damaging your spirits and what little bit of courage you had before, when you thought you had life figured out.

So, my suggestion to you is that you define life and define yourself in the process. Break down what you don't understand into manageable chunks until you have it figured out. Take baby steps, research words you don't know and study things you do want to know. My final task for you is to come up with at least one sentence that defines what life means to you and make that sentence applicable to your life.

Lastly, see if you can fill in the blank here:

1) Life means _____ to me! I know this is true because when I apply _____ to my life, it makes me feel _____.

   No one else can define what your life means to you more than you can. Applying that definition to your world on a day-to-day basis will only boost your confidence in knowing what life means to you.

Chapter 2
What Does Life Coaching Yourself Mean?

Life coaching yourself means to take control of what is yours. Life offers everyone the same opportunities but not everyone goes after them in the same way or with the same passion. Some waste no time achieving everything, while others waste every day achieving nothing. Life has ups and downs that will knock us off our journey; but to get back up and claim what is yours is achieving more than enough.

When writing this book, I asked one of my younger sisters, aka sissy, "What does life mean to you?" and her response was "Everything"—nothing more and nothing less. Maybe that is enough. I don't know. But to have that mentality means that you know where you want to go and you know that you need to take measures to get there. But sometimes the heights are too high to climb. So, what now? You lose motivation because you begin to think that what you want is unrealistic.

Life can be so meaningful if you know the direction you want to go in. On the flip side, life can be so painful if you keep walking in the wrong direction. To life coach yourself, you need to know what you want out of life, know where you can go to get it, and know the costs and consequences to achieving it. This is the first step to life coaching yourself into what you want.

Some people let life pass them by because they are content, but what people don't realize is that life coaching yourself can never stop because the opportunities never cease. To achieve everything and avoid losing it all, you have to keep coaching yourself on how to be successful, as well as how to maintain that success. It is important for you to coach yourself as often as you can to learn as much as you can. The moment you stop coaching yourself, that is the minute others grab what could have been yours.

For example, if you take time to sleep on an idea for, say, a week or two, have you ever wondered how much time you could lose waiting? In one week alone, one could make a fortune selling your idea to another person or company. By two weeks, two more people can make the same fortune each selling your idea to another two companies. Now within that week that you have been pondering your next move and sleeping on your idea, you have made someone you shared your idea with three times richer than you. But, if you begin life coaching yourself today into what your heart desires, you can avoid missing your opportunity to succeed. If you can begin coaching yourself today on making the next best move, then you could find your dream staying with you and financially, in your pocket.

So, my suggestions to you are that first, keep your dream close to your heart, and second, learn how to coach yourself to take control of what life has to offer you now, not tomorrow. Tomorrow's opportunities are not guaranteed today.

Lastly, ask yourself this question below:

1) What does life coaching yourself mean to you?

_____

_____

_____

Chapter 3
Do You Trust Yourself?

In order to be comfortable with the choices you make in life or the direction you would like to take lead or go in, you have to trust your instincts from within to make sound decisions regarding anything and everything.

As I am sitting on the deck of the Starbucks on the Corner of Ocean Drive in Miami writing this chapter, I notice that people are going in different directions: some are going to my right and some are going to my left, some are not sure where they want to go. It had me thinking several different things. One, when people think they know the direction they want to go in or they are leading, it appears they do not. Two, when people seem to be unclear of the direction they need to go rather than want to go in, they sometimes have to go back in the other direction to start all over again. By default, they will end up back where they started. Regardless if it's a need or want, people sometimes cannot figure out which direction is perfect for their life. Three, when people appear to be lost, by the look on their face or their body language, they end up having a conniption because they thought they knew themselves well enough to have their directions all figured out.

In an attempt to make my point more clear, let me say this again: When people seem to be unclear of which direction they want to go in life, they sometimes have to go back in the opposite direction to start all over again. In this case they end up at the same place they originally started because they didn't trust their own judgment from the get go.

In life you have to learn to trust your own instincts. You have to trust yourself to find your way through decisions. That may take bobbing and weaving through different paths until you find the right one for you. Sometimes it may seem so hard or confusing to find that right path for yourself but in order to get past that doubt, you have to trust yourself. You have to trust your inner feelings to allow you to have good in your life. You also have to trust your inner feeling to know when it is clear that something or someone is leading you in a bad situation and when there is a need to avoid negativity that can lead you in the wrong direction.

You have to know that, without direction, anyone can fail, and with direction, many can succeed. I once heard that if you know the direction you are going in, then you could find your way. Sometimes it is going to seem like you don't know your left from your right when you are faced with a decision, but sometimes you also have to learn how to allow your gut feelings to help you make the right decision. Following your gut can be a huge indicator for what is right and what is wrong. I hear people sometimes say that you need to go with your heart over your mind and go with your mind over your gut.

Sometimes I find it hard to trust my mind over my gut and after several failed experiences of not trusting myself, I learned to trust my gut to steer me in the right direction. I honestly do not believe that is easy to do. For example, you can allow your mind to make a bad decision for you but your gut will never steer you wrong. There have been times when my mind would try to take over my gut feeling while I was driving and trying to find my destination. I remember during one specific time when I was driving, my mind was telling me to go in a specific direction, but my gut was telling me that direction didn't look right, so I took an alternate route and ended up in the right place two hours later. I initially thought it was hard to trust my mind because you always think the first thing you want to use when you are trying to find a place is your mind, right? Well in this case it wasn't needed! My point is that when you get in situations like this; you will know when it's best to use your gut over your mind.

In another example, you can allow your heart to also make a bad judgment for you, but again, your gut will never lead you a stray. In fact your gut and your heart can react from the same feelings when you trust another person with your heart. I remember a time when I trusted my heart with someone else, as a love language or symbol of love. This person was someone I loved dearly and thought I was destined to be with forever. In my heart, I knew he loved me and in my gut I genuinely knew he felt the same way. At that time, my gut and heart were reacting off the same feelings because of love. It wasn't until later when I learned to trust myself by reevaluating the negative signs that were displayed before me, that my gut feelings began to change. As I grew stronger with my instincts and by trusting myself, my gut began to show me that although this person loved me genuinely, they didn't treat me the way I deserved to be treated. In this case, my gut won over my mind. Never forget that your mind, heart, and gut can blindside you if you don't know how to trust yourself first.

I believe people trust themselves to go in a specific direction for three reasons: comfort, familiarity, and to get answers. Without these three things they would be dreading going to an unfamiliar territory, uncomfortable directions and a place with no answers.

So, my suggestion to you is that you have to learn how to trust yourself completely before making decisions, but be smart and don't miss out on opportunities because of a wrong judgment call. This is very important to remember when you are determining which life path is right for you.

Lastly, honestly ask yourself "Do You Trust Yourself" (the direction I am going in or the life I am leading)?

Attempt to fill in the blanks below:

1) I trust myself to do _____. I know this is true because I never _____ an opportunity when it becomes available to me.

Chapter 4
Know What Your Purpose Is In Life

When you find something you want to do in life, don't let anything stop you and go for it. You need to figure out how to overcome the challenges that may come your way. You have to build the will power to stay focused on what it is you want in life. Sometimes that starts by holding true to your vision. According to John Maxwell (2010), "Anyone can follow a path, but only a leader can blaze one" (p. v). Holding true to your vision can begin with having leadership abilities. If you are one who already possesses leadership skills, then that takes you one step closer to finding what you want to do in life. Currently, if you think you are one who does not possess enough leadership skills to determine what you want in life, then reading this chapter and chapter 6 will help you get there.

Leaders usually know what they want to be and how they are going to get there before they even get there. Leaders possess a vision for their journey that only they can bring to life. This is why it's important to know what you want in life and to keep your focus on it until you get there.

I spent many nights writing this book and many others because I had a vision. I remained so loyal to my vision that I would take napkins from anywhere I could to write on and plenty of colorful pens to write with everywhere I went, all because I had a vision. Nothing was getting in the way of my writing. No distance, no drive, no forgotten supplies! I always want to be prepared at all times, since I have a vision for everything that I want to do or associate myself with in my life. Same with my book review website. I had a vision to put as many books up as I could on a site for less fortunate readers to read prior to purchasing. I looked at it like this: I was already finishing a book manuscript every week anyway, why not make someone else happy by sharing what I knew or had read? At the time that was my vision. While both visions have been successful, there was still one problem: I had too many visions, and to this day I still do. There are some days my brain never sleeps and I've come to the realization that there may not be a way to overcome that, because I am always coming up with more goals that I want to accomplish in life. At an early age, I became obsessed with learning and self-educating myself. In fact, that has been my drug of choice for years. My family may say working is my addiction drug of choice because they see me working around the clock. However, the truth is that when I do what I love, it soothes me; working is sometimes my warm shoulder to cry on.

In the fall of 2010, I had the pleasure of speaking with Sharon Flake (a well-known and established author of several successful books including *The Skin I'm In* and *Begging for Change*). She told me that while I already had many manuscripts completed, I needed to focus on writing one good book. That little advice was one of the best suggestions I had received in a long time when it came to writing. Sharon Flake was already a successful publisher (which is where I wanted to be), so I trusted her advice. She disclosed to me that to date, she had sold over 600,000 copies of her first book, and many books later, she is still a successful author, so why wouldn't I trust her advice? (In later chapters I will explain how using resources is so important in getting where you want to be in life.) The advice that she gave me will take me a long way to writing many books later. Before speaking to Sharon, I was sort of lost; I did not know which book I wanted to publish first, which story would be a hit, and which would not.

I had a vision for a children's series to be my first book to be released for three years prior to its drop date. Sometimes, our vision is interrupted because of things that are out of our reach and as a result we are forced to focus on a different vision. So, in the meantime, I had decided to take time preparing my second manuscript (which is this book) for its own release date, while I had to put "Where did my half-brother come from" on a hiatus. Although I went through so many complications to birth my first series, it still became my first book to be released in 2012.

Sometimes in life you have to alter your vision to make things happen for yourself. I believe it's a good thing when you know all the things that you want to achieve in life because you have the opportunity to alternate some of those things, based on life's circumstances or things that are out of your control. Altering your vision does not mean that your current vision will never come to light; it just means it's not the right time to birth that vision. At that point, it is okay to be smart and stay clear of the warning signs that show it may not be your time to start a new project (i.e., other things could be soaking up your focus).

Knowing what you want is sometimes about discovering what you truly want out of life, what your heart desires the most. As a life coach and doctor, in addition to other counseling/life coaching methods, I often use the Reality Therapy Model with my clients. I have found that this method helps my clients discover more than their wants, but also their desire to change and find their purpose in life. Reality therapy is used to help clients also gain control over their life (Wubbolding, 2000). I find that my clients enjoy this model over anything else because it helps them to choose only behaviors they find desirable to change, fix, or accomplish versus those behaviors that are not desirable.

So, my suggestion to you is that you take time to determine what dreams, goals, and aspirations your heart desires to accomplish. Keep in mind that you can have many visions of what you want to do in life, however it is best to focus on one vision until you can see it through to the end. This will help you avoid being scattered with your ideas.

Lastly, ask yourself these questions below:

1) What is My Purpose in Life?

_____

_____

_____

2) Am I going after desirable behaviors that will help me find my purpose in life?

_____

_____

_____

Chapter 5
Dare To Dream But Don't Strive For Another's Dream

Dreaming in life is a part of growing and living. We all are capable of dreaming. Sometimes it can be a stress reliever and we often do it more than we expect to or even acknowledge. Either way, it is important to know why you are dreaming, whether you are doing it as a habit or to determine where you want to be in life. It is very common to dream of our future often. It is also okay to dream as a remedy, but my point is this: Know why you are dreaming!

Often, when we are dreaming, it is because we may need to make or foresee a change in our life is needed and that is why we are dreaming beyond our current circumstance. Maybe we are just dreaming for something we also desire or want to take place in our life.

Sometimes we also get the same vision from our sleeping dreams. For example, have you ever had a dream that symbolizes death? According to Altman (2002), this is a reminder that you have limited time for personal fulfillment or that you may be under pressure to meet a strict deadline. Most of the time when you dream one thing, it means another. I have done so much research on dreams and purchased so many books on dreams that I have learned there are levels in dreaming. For example, dreaming about dying and dreaming about death can be interpreted very differently. According to Dream Moods (2017), dreaming of death should not be taken as referring to a physical death; it is more of a sign that something in your waking life is either ending or changing. Whether you have limited time for personal fulfillment, must meet a strict deadline, or are facing a life change event, don't be afraid to interpret your dream because it is a step toward understanding your life and possibly a sign of where you want to be in life.

Just like you have to be sure you know what you want to do in life, you also have to make sure that you know that whatever you decide to do or try to accomplish this is something only you TRULY WANT. Sometimes we get caught up in following other people's dreams. We listen to others (i.e., family, friends, and associates) tell their dream as if they are selling it to us and we fall for what they want (instead of focusing on what WE want). When sharing their plan with us, they propose their ideas to us so well that we feel like they are asking us to be a partner; a part of their dream, and although they haven't asked us anything, we still get caught up mentally tricking ourselves into believing this notion. Another thing is when they are sharing their dreams with us and showing how they have everything mapped out so well, it also makes it easier for us to want to take part in that dream that was never ours to begin with. Or shall I say, we begin to take part of that dream for ourselves without them even offering or asking us to. Why not? It makes life easier! Their plan is already made up! So, we force feed our mentality to believe that their plan can and should be our dream too.

The problem is that if it's not your dream, it will fail. What's for you is for you and what's for someone else is for them. God has a plan for everyone and he predestines your thoughts and plans uniquely to fit you and only you. Tyrese (the R & B Artist) stated something similar to this in his book How to Get Out of Your Own Way. In fact, now that I am reading his book, it reminds me a lot of the advice I gave out in this book. So, it's cool that I can go back and fill in other's quotes where I have stated similar things. It drives my point even closer to home for you as my reader. So, in his book, Tyrese stated, "every time you get an idea it's a blessing from God (…) you're channeling God's idea, something that he sent to you. And God would never give you something somebody else is supposed to have" (Gibson, 2011, p. 217).

Have you ever seen someone try to make a dream happen and they fail midway through because they didn't have the entire plan together? Another problem is that they only had some of the details of the other person's dream mixed in with their half-planned dream. Understand this, people who make things happen in their life do not share their real dreams with the world before the goal is completed. The reason is because they don't want to seem like their plan is half-baked before it is cooked completely. In addition, they don't want to become that person who does not get the opportunity to see their dreams come true, because they are living another person's dream.

If your dream belongs to you, make sure it stays with you. Don't allow others to ruin, steal, or alter your dream to make it their dream. This is the first step in allowing yourself not to strive for someone else's dream. The same goes for you! Do not take another person's dream to make your dream complete. In other words, learn how to detect when something is for you and when something is not! If an idea of a dream belongs to someone else, let it stay with that person. Instead, focus on what is yours to believe in and what is not. If you don't know how to do that, think like this, if it's your dream, it's for you, therefore you should be the one to see it through. Do not get caught up in thinking someone else's dream is for you just because you heard it. For this reason, you want to avoid letting other peoples' dreams intertwine or mix with yours. One of the worst things in life is being blasted for stealing someone else's dream. Secondly, this is why it is important to focus and follow through on your dream and your dream only.

In the book, titled *A Tap Water Girl in a Bottled Water World*, Shirley Garrett (2002), the author and my speaking coach, shared a point in her life when she discovered she would never be like the other women she once desired to be like. She was happy being herself because she said it took a full-time job just being who she already was without the added pressure of being like someone else. When I read this in Shirley's book I realize when someone is trying to be bigger than who they currently are, it becomes more than just a full-time job. Being someone else takes much more work ethics than being who you already are and destined to become. Even reading this short manual and applying these methods to your life will be more work than you probably anticipate because there are new things that you did not know or have done before. Just as it was hard work for me to write this book because of not only the time it took to write it, but also the work it also took to edit, re-edit, and send to professionals to re-edit and the illustrators, etc. My point is that it takes work to be who you are and who you want to become. Never loose site of who God has intended for you to be. Shirley also stated in her book that when she realized this discovery above, the moment had come where she decided she would be who she was intended to be, a tap water girl in a bottled water world and through this discovery she acknowledged who she was and who she was not. I think that is the best lesson anyone can learn that you are who you are, and you cannot be anyone that you are not meant to be! Remember, God created us uniquely special to do what we are put on this Earth to do.

Another thing, avoid living your life for someone else. For example, if it's your parents and they ask you to do, build, create, plan or go after something they always wanted you to do, think about who you are doing it for before making that dream your dream. Sometimes our parents or other influential people in our life may say "I always wanted that for you" or "I am so glad you are finally seeing my dreams through." This is all fine and dandy but first, make sure it is your dream too. You don't want to seem like more of a failure because you didn't fulfill your parents' dream. The pressure to press forward will seem impossible, as well as the expectations to succeed. In the book *Kardashian Konfidential,* one of the sisters stated, "You can't make everyone happy, you just have to try to make yourself happy" (Kardashian, Kardashian, & Kardashian, 2010, p. 143). That is what it's all about, making you happy and only you. You really cannot make anyone else happy until you make yourself happy. This is the third step in learning how to strive for your own dream.

Michael Baisden recently stated on his radio show (aired in Miami Florida on Hot 105.1 FM) that there are going to be people who will not understand what you are trying to accomplish in life. He shared that there were people who did not believe he could be an author and radio personality, but he stayed faithful to his dreams and became one of the most popular authors and radio personalities today. He quoted "Do not let anyone rob you of your dreams. Do something creative or you will never be happy" (Baisden, 2012).

So, my suggestion to you is that you focus on making yourself happy by going after what it is that YOU want. Never allow others to alter your direction with their ideas of what they believe is the best career path for you. Only you can determine what it is YOU want and desire. So live your life for you and avoid dreaming for others.

Don't get caught up competing with others for their dreams either. Remember, God will only give you a dream to birth because it is for you. He will never give you an idea, dream, or vision for someone else.

Lastly, ask yourself these two questions:

1) What is my dream?

_____

_____

_____

2) Is my dream for me because it fulfills me and not anyone else's?

_____

_____

_____

Chapter 6
Think Like A Leader To Become One

When you are trying to figure out what direction to take in life, you have to think in terms of being a leader. Leadership is built from within. You either possess the skills to be a leader or you do not. Have you ever heard that saying, "there are two kinds of people in this world, a leader and a follower," or the one where people say "there are two kinds of people in this world, those that make things happen and those that let things happen." Well either you guide or you can be guided by someone else. A leader differs from a follower because they have the desire to lead and make things happen for themselves, whereas, a follower looks to follow or for someone else to guide them because they do not possess the skills to lead themselves in any direction, even if it is one that they desire!

A follower also allows things to happen without having a say-so or voice to change them. How can they with no instructions on how to do so or the personal instinct to make things happen as a leader?

To be successful in life you have to get in the race and lead your life in the direction that you would like it to go in. You cannot sit around, write all these goals down, set plans to proceed and just fall back until someone shows you your next step. Rather, you have to know your next step and lead yourself there. How will you show others what you are capable of doing if you are not leading? Have you ever seen the lead performer or singer in a show wait for others to give the cue before they make a move? Absolutely not! No way! If everyone is waiting on the leader to give the cue for them to begin, whom would the leader be waiting on? That person is the leader and normally they do a good job at leading others. If you are a leader you already possess the skills to lead others; therefore you should embrace it and not avoid it (sometimes leaders fail to lead on purpose because of their own issues with guiding), but if you are not as sharp as your average leader, then this chapter can help you learn to take the lead in your life decisions. Even if you are a leader that already possesses the leadership skill, you can still get confused with guiding others so this chapter can still help you learn other ways to take the lead in your life.

It is time for you to educate yourself on how to be a leader altogether. The same goes for success. If you want to be prosperous, you have to think like a leader and go after what you want. You have to take control of your life and lead yourself right to that success and prosperity. If you are thinking as a leader, you are not waiting for anyone's suggestions, advice, warnings, or ideas on how you should lead your life. Instead, you are making sound decisions on your own as a leader.

Understand that when you begin to trust yourself, you take the lead in driving your own life down this path of leadership. Keep in mind that a true leader stays determined to make progress. As a leader you have to continue to focus and avoid destructiveness at all costs. Dr. John Maxwell stated in his leadership devotional journal that a leader is one who can stand up in a crisis. They have a positive focus and they refuse to dwell on destructive issues. Instead they focus on becoming pure; they discipline their mind to remain clean and pure (Maxwell, 2011, p. 6). This is the beginning of guiding your life into leadership!

So my suggestion to you is that when you think and know what you want to do in life, you need to dwell on it until it happens, but also make leadership moves in the process to get you there. Trust yourself to make decisions to get there, even if you are not sure. How will you know if it's right or not if you don't try it? Whether it's right depends on how you take the results. Part of being a leader is making decisions that no one else will or wants to make, whether they're good or bad. The results of these types of decisions could end up being lessons learned for you and your followers. No one is perfect and not everyone makes good decisions all the time and that is okay. Sometimes making bad decisions allow us to make better decisions later on. So do not get discouraged if you happen to make a bad decision or two one time or another. Remember, above all, if you look at yourself as a leader, others will too and they will respect your decisions. In the end, this could be a lesson learned for others to follow your lead.

Lastly, ask yourself these two questions:

1) Are you thinking like a leader when it comes to running and implementing your business goals?

_____

_____

_____

2) Are you taking the right steps to thinking and becoming a leader towards your personal goals?

_____

_____

_____

Chapter 7
Understand Failing Is Only The Beginning

As an individual and a leader trying to understand what you want to gain out of life, you will make some decisions that will fall through, but that doesn't quite mean you've failed and it's the end. It just means that you will simply pick up the pieces and do it all over again but with a different focus or technique. Failing can mean a lot of things. The *Merriam-Webster Online Dictionary* (2012) defines failing as a "slight or insignificant defect in character, conduct, or ability." Based on this definition, one is not a flat-out failure but more of someone with a slight inability to succeed or imperfection in their character. We all have something not perfect about us, but that does not mean we are failures. It just means that we are not perfect and we are all built to fail. Everyone you know or come across is bound to fail at one time or another in life. John Maxwell stated, "God uses people who fail—cause there aren't any other kinds around" (Maxwell, 2000, p. 27). Do you think you are an exception?

According to the *Merriam-Webster Online Dictionary* (2012), a failure is defined as "omission of occurrence or performance; a state of inability to perform a normal function; lack of success; a failing business; a falling short." Based on this definition, a person who has an off day can be considered a failure. A person who lacks the ability to function normally on a day-to-day basis can also be a failure, based on this definition; but does that mean it has to last or that person's "off day" will be permanent? No! Of course not!

Have you ever had a day where things were just not going right for you? Yes! Of course! We all have! My aunt always says when you have days like this "Just go back to bed and try again tomorrow." That's what it's about: getting back up when you have failed. As mentioned in the last chapter, no one is exempt from making a good or bad decision. How you handle it is what is more important. One of the best lessons you can learn in life is that in order to prevail over failure, you to accept the results that you receive as a learning curve. You have to learn something new from each failed experience and look at each one of those experiences as something worth learning. This is the first step to understanding that when you fail, it does not mean your life is over.

A term I like to share often with my clients that I learned in my life coaching certification program is that there is no such thing as failure, only feedback! You have to look at every failed experience as feedback. If you don't feel comfortable doing that, you can ask yourself, if I don't fail, then how can I learn? Sometimes trial and error is effective for some of the decisions you make in life because it is the only way you will know what will work and what will not work in your life.

Another way to learn from failing is through reflection. When you fail, you have to reflect on the reasons behind why you failed to avoid it from happening the same way again. Reflecting on what caused your plan to fail can be powerful and can make a difference in how you view your failure. You cannot let it devalue who you are and your abilities. Sometimes we let failure determine how successful we want to be. If we have failed at something, we allow it to discourage us from making even higher goals. We cannot let one experience affect our original goals or devalue our knowledge and worth. We did not spend countless months self-educating ourselves to fail. So why stop here because of a little bump in the road? John Maxwell stated that we should always make a habit of involving ourselves in the things we are mostly afraid of, and that if we do this, our fear of that thing will die (Maxwell, 2000).

Another way to use reflection to help you move past a failed experience is to evaluate your current goals and determine where you need to make changes in your life. You should reflect quietly, consciously and figuratively in order to capture a true reflection of your failed experience. Your main goal should be to understand why you failed, learn from it, and fix it. Reflection can be our best teacher sometimes. If you can change how you view failure from this experience, then you will be able to see the vision destined for your life.

Once you pick yourself up from your failed experience, regardless of what it was, you have to learn how to forgive yourself and move on from it. It is almost the same process as learning how to let go of things that are out of your control (covered in Chapter 16), which is also learning how to forgive yourself and moving beyond that experience.

How you respond to others after a failed experience is also an important step in moving beyond your failed experiences. One thing you need to keep in mind when it comes to learning how to move beyond either experiences, remember there will always be others who enjoy reminding you of how hard you failed, when they see you, but it will be you that have to put an end to this type of unwanted attention. You have to stop these individuals in their tracks and tell them you are in a different space, you have moved on from that situation and are now doing better things in your life (that can be later discussed at your will).

I read in a *Sister 2 Sister Magazine* (February 2012 issue) Interview with Clifford "T. I." Harris who during the interview was expressing his frustration for often being ridiculed by others about his experiences before, diurng and after he served time in jail in 2009 and 2010–2011. He stated "It's so many other things that I consist of" (rather than discuss his faults or the fact that he went to jail every time he does an interview or someone sees him) (p. 59). Whenever you are faced with the same type of frustration because others cannot let you forget when and how you fail at something, you have to handle it just as firm and clear as Mr. Harris did in this interview. Although his frustration was directed towards those who are caught up in discussing things related to his jail sentence, he did not direct that frustration to the person who did his interview (Jamie Foster) but to those who were reading it and still relate the experience to the status quo of his life. I see it this way: Sometimes you have to fail in order to succeed! T.I. also mentioned in the same interview that everyone goes through some type of turmoil at one point or another in their life, and these experiences can help build one's character and strength. In other words, what don't kill you will definitely make you stronger! We cannot go through nothing and in return expect something! We have to go through something in life to get more than nothing out of life! I always believe that in order to be someone big in life, you have to go through something in life!

Just remember that when there are others who want to remind you that you have failed, you have to show them that that was only the beginning of your success and that you too have more things in life that you consist of that can be up for discussion at your expense only. Meaning it is up to you to discuss at your own will and time!

I believe how you bounce back from your failure is more important and more of a joy than the pain you experienced when you were failing. I recently read in an *Ebony Magazine* (The Black Wealth July 2012 Issue) where Steve Harvey had a similar thought, and where he dished out eight principles to making millions. Principle number 4 was titled "Bounce Back From Failure" and under this principle, Steve Harvey explains how he went from having no income in 2005 because his TV Show "The Steve Harvey Show" had been canceled. He had no comedy acts scheduled, and he had walked away from a $7 million radio deal to start his own radio program but because he had determination to make it, he did. Steve quoted in that interview "You may fail, but you are not a failure if you're learning. When you learn, you grow. That's how it's done. I don't care how many times you have to keep getting up; if you stay down; it's over. Keep putting one foot in front of the other. Shake the naysayers. Quit talking to the haters. They have nothing to do with your future. They don't know what your plan is" (p. 105).

So my suggestion to you is if you fail at something you've poured your heart and time into, understand why you have failed and move past it. Failed experiences are meant to force us to work harder and get more!

Lastly, ask yourself these questions below:

1) What have you learned from your failed experiences that is going to help you move forward?

_____
_____
_____

2) What are the positive steps you are taking to move beyond your failed experiences?

_____

_____

_____

Chapter 8
Check Out Your Competition

There is no secret to how many people compete with others for a living. Competition is all around us: in our work place, children's daycare, at the bank, and in the department stores. Sometimes we can lose focus on our goals in life because of competition. In the past decade, competition has really taken a toll on our standards and expectations of others. Everywhere you go, you see some form of competition. For example, some days I see women who are thrilled at the opportunity to show they have excelled at something and are past the next female. I also see guys happy to have something materialistic to show the next male, just because they have the same opportunity (as some women do, in the example above) to show they've got it. On the other hand, children fight for attention from their parents, siblings, teachers, classmates, and friends. No matter how you describe it, it exists and sometimes we allow it to eat at us. Most of the time when this happens, it is unbeknownst to us and probably to our competitor too. Competing has become so frequent in our society that often times we are not aware of when it takes place; but one thing for sure is that we allow it to alter our thinking and how we perceive our goals.

For example, do you ever stand in line at a fast food restaurant and realize someone else in that line (maybe another person of the same gender) is checking you out like they have something slick or condescending to say to you, but when they see you looking, they act like they are better than you and weren't even thinking about you! When this happens, I feel like they are rudely looking up and down at me to see where my status is in life. I have very low tolerance for this behavior. However, there are other ways to checking out your competition without sizing them up. Sometimes it is important for us to check out our competition for learning purposes rather than checking to see what another person has in their possession.

Competition is not about what one has and how well they flaunt it, but rather it is about congratulating someone on their success by the way they carry themselves or even by silently recognizing their clean look. When you look at another person with hatred and jealousy, you are showing how insecure you are in yourself. You are actually speaking out loud to others, letting them know you are not happy with who you are and where you want to be in life. You cannot allow your competition to reel you in about the wrong things. It's wasted energy and it takes away from accomplishing your goals. Regardless of how big or small the goal may be (i.e., buying a new car, changing jobs, finding a sitter, etc.); you have to stay focused on what you are fighting for right now in your life.

As I was finishing up Jay Z's book titled *Decoded* while writing part of this book, I found so many valuable quotes on competition. So, excuse me if this chapter seems longer than the others, but I have to share a few good examples of how one should understand competition.

The first quote that stood out for me in Jay Z's *Decoded* is very helpful in understanding the message I am trying to convey in this chapter. Jay Z stated that a "competition pushes you to become your best self, and in the end it tells you where you stand" (Carter, 2010, p. 71). You have to remember what you are fighting for and why you are in this fight in the first place by keeping your eye on the ultimate goal of success.

In order to move ahead with your future goals, you always need to know your competitor's position. This is an important step in learning how to check out your competition. You want to know in advance who you feel is going to try to stop you from getting ahead. In this game of life and success, you need to know who is currently getting ahead and who does not plan to share their territory with you in your area of interest. According to Kimberly Seals-Allers, who is the author of the *Mocha Manual,* when it comes to your competition, "You want to stand out in the crowd, not blend into the pack" (2009, p. 167). You want to clearly define your position from your competitor's position and set yourself apart from them, even if you two can relate, because at the end of the day, you two are still competing for the winning spot, the same and best invention and investment. You want to always be on your "A Game" when it comes to challenging your competition, to show you are confident in what you know and what you are planning to do.

Checking out your competitor can mean so many things and be done for so many positive reasons. The main thing is that you want to learn from your competitors. I read in a *JET Magazine* Interview (July 23, 2012 issue) that Earvin "Magic" Johnson currently has a new network name "Aspire." During the interview, Magic was asked if he had looked at the Oprah Winfrey Model (for her network) prior to building his own network and his response was "I will continue to look at it because you have to learn from others" (p. 24). I believe he meant that in order for us to learn from others in the industry we are interested in going into, we have to start somewhere and usually that begins with looking at someone who has already succeeded in that specific industry. This is what "checking out your competition" is about! Nothing more and nothing less!

My point is that you have to think of positive reasons as to why you check out your competition. My purpose has always been ONLY to learn and determine what works, what does not work and how I can make an impact to deliver what is missing in my industry. Although your reasons for checking out your competition may vary, your overall goal should be positive. Otherwise, alternative motives will cause you to fail.

So, my suggestion to you is that you need to have a goal when dealing with your competitors, whether it's to learn something or running a race to the top against them. Jay Z also mentioned in *Decoded* (Carter, 2010) that he competes with himself, because it pushes him to work harder for what he wants in life. Try to do the same for yourself and one way to learn more about yourself and what you want to accomplish in life is to compete with yourself and see if it brings you out on top every time.

Lastly, ask yourself these questions below:

1) What is the best way to compete with myself to come out on top every time?

_____

_____

_____

2) How can I check out my competitor in a way that it keeps me focused on succeeding at my ultimate goal?

   _____

   _____

   _____

3) What can I learn from my competitor that will help me to excel in my industry?

   _____

   _____

   _____

Chapter 9
Utilize Your Resources

When you are trying to connect with others who are successful in your field or area of interest, you need to approach them with confidence. Prior to reaching out, you need to know who is successful in your area and who is not. This is your first step to learning how to use your resources. There are some individuals who portray themselves as having the lifestyle and success you want versus those who really have the life style you are aspiring to live and be like. Either way, you need to be aware of those individuals to determine to whom is a more reliable resource.

This brings me to the next step in using your resources. If I had one short word of advice in how to use your resources it would be to STUDY. Take some time and begin studying where you want to be in life! Even if it is just following a new weight-management plan, buying a new car or investing in property. You also need to be aware of the pitfalls that often take place in your new interests to avoid a quick let down. Finally, you need to become resourceful when it comes to finding and using your personal resources.

In this day and age, it is evident that we can use technology to help us become resourceful, but to get where you want to be in your life, you need to network with others who will help you to grow and learn. These two things are key factors in using your resources. For example, say you want to learn how to be more prominent in your new line of work, do you think you will get there by just sitting at home or going out into the community mingling here and there? Let me answer that for you: it will take you being proactive, going out and showing your face for others to have something to remember you by, basically allowing others to put a name with your face.

Ideally, when a person meets you, they should be able to remember you if you left them with something memorable of yourself that explains why you stand out from others. The same would go for someone you meet who is already prominent in their field. You should know as many details as you can gather about that person prior to having a two minute conversation with them. Sometimes that is all the time you are given to tell who you are when meeting someone prominent. Believe me, every second counts, so make use of it by gathering as much information as you can and don't forget to dish out as much information as you can too, if you are given the opportunity to verbalize your interests, ideas, and or business plans to that same person. When you use your resources, you want people to never forget about you. As the late Tupac Shakur (2003) stated in one of his documentaries, Resurrection, "Either you evolve or disappear." This really means that you either take an opportunity like this and make use of it or do not bother wasting another person's time (basically go home). Jay Z also stated something similar in his book, *Decoded* (Carter, 2010), that everyone deserves the opportunity to evolve when you are given the opportunity to do so. However, prior to doing this, you have to make a decision on whether you want to make use of your time and others' time effectively or go home! No if, ands, or buts about it! If you can use the opportunity that is given to you, regardless of whether it's five minutes or 1 minute, make it your debut! But in order to do this, you need to seize the opportunity at the time that it is given. This brings me back to emphasizing how important it is to use your resources when you have the opportunity to do so.

Another way to do this is by understanding others' purpose in your life (see Chapter 10) and by checking out your competition (see Chapter 8). If you really want to use the resources that are close to you, think about all the people in your circle (who you can trust), who have the skills you are looking for to help you complete your personal projects. For example, one of the editors I used for this book was referred to me through a chain of emails from another editor. Originally, I had no idea this reference (professional editor) would come through a different resource. But guess what? All it took was for me to network, be open and clear as to what I was looking for in an editor at the time the opportunity was given to me. Utilizing your resources is also about sharing the right information with the right person at the right time.

So, my suggestion to you is, as you are moving to the top, think of someone who can help you expand your resources and in the end help you save financially to launch your plans. Also, remember when you're thinking about how to use your resources, consider those who are not in your social circle or directly on your team but do possess the qualities you are looking for and are willing to help you succeed. As the Kardashian sisters put it in their latest book "capitalize on your opportunities" (2010, p. 214); you want to do this as often as you can and as much as you can. This is the last step in learning how to use your resources.

If I can leave you with anything from this chapter, it would be a quote from our current and first Black President's book *The Audacity of Hope* remember "it is not just our natural resources that account for our economic success but also our system of social organization, a system that for generations has encouraged constant innovation, individual initiative, and the efficient allocation of resources" that are often offered to us in our lifetime (Obama, 2006, p. 150).

Lastly, when you are thinking of ways you can utilize your resources, ask yourself this question below:

1) What resources are available to me and how can I use those resources to capitalize on more opportunities that are available for me?

_____

_____

_____

Chapter 10
Understand Others' Purpose In Your Life

People come and go in your life for several reasons that may be unbeknownst to you and to them. Reflecting on someone's role in your life can be the first step to understanding why another person has been destined to come across your path. If you can understand that, you can make sense of a lot of things that take place in your life, even in a stuck situation. Sometimes it also takes feeling that other person out, or scoping him/her out for any relation to you before understanding another person's purpose in your life. Sometimes it takes hearing someone else tell you the truth about yourself before you begin to believe in your purpose and trust yourself. Think about it! Let me give you a snippet of how I had a lesson to learn on understanding someone's purpose in my life.

Very recently, I was wandering around Collins Avenue in the Miami South Beach area looking for a Wi-Fi Café. I ran into a guy who physically appeared to be homeless, but instantly caught my attention because he asked me a question about my childhood and then another about love. Next thing you know, he was telling me things that had taken place in my past and current life, he even went as far as to begin saying things that would take place in my future! What scared me the most was that he was speaking to me as if he already knew me! The things that he was saying really had me stuck in thought! After a while I was looking at him sideways, because he had reeled me in like a salt-water fish for bait. I was so shocked that he knew so much about me. He didn't have any rhyme or reason, documents or degrees to account for his knowledge but his information was on point. My point is you never know why people come into your life. Sometimes it can be to help you re-evaluate your journey, which is exactly what this situation did for me at the time.

As a life coach I reach out to many people that God puts in my path to help because he knows I am good with inspiring and understanding others. However, this particular day was meant for someone to be put in my path to help me. Looking back on it now, this guy was probably no bum but an involuntarily psychic with natural instincts. This goes to show you that we should never judge a book by its cover! With that said, allow yourself to trust others when they come into your life because you never know what purpose they may serve. By being unaware, you can turn down good help and be stuck in the same position for twenty more years. Or you can allow someone to come in and help you understand things differently.

So, my suggestion to you is that you have to not only use your resources, regardless of how they are delivered to you, but you also have to understand the purpose of your resource's position in your life. While I never agreed to see a psychic in the past, it was evident that on this day one was meant to see me. His truths racked my brain and hit my heart so heavily, it had me reacting, responding, and preparing. People come into our lives for many different reasons, sometimes we want change but don't know how soon we can get it until we open the door and let someone in to help us.

As mentioned in the last chapter, use your resources to figure out another person's purpose in your life. Last fall, Arsenio Hall was on one of Oprah's shows called the "Next Runner Up" on OWN (Hall, 2011) and he told two contestants during an elimination that "There's something special about all of us; know what that is and work towards that." Oftentimes it takes other people to come into our lives to help us figure out our own purpose in life. If needed, you can go back and review chapter 4, where I discussed how and why you need to know your purpose in life.

Remember, you have to know your purpose in order to fulfill your passion. If you are not sure what your passion is, then you will have an even more difficult time discovering what your existence on this Earth means and why you were put here. For example, I believe that my purpose in life is to help others get where they need and want to be in life. That is why I am writing this book and that is why I am a life coach. I recently heard Hosea Chanchez mention in an interview that his passion allowed him to fulfill his purpose and that he also believes that a person's purpose is always fulfilled with someone else. If you don't get anything else from this chapter, remember that when you determine how to fulfill your purpose, you will want to put the passion behind it, in order for it to come to life.

Lastly, think about other people who have come into your life and ask yourself these questions below:

1) What is the purpose God has placed each of those individuals into your life?

_____
_____
_____

2) How can this relate to my desire to be successful?

_____
_____
_____

Chapter 11
Determine Who Is On Your Team

Determining who has a positive impact on your team can be hard. Let's begin with understanding what the word **T.E.A.M.** stands for in general. My definition of **T.E.A.M.** stands for **T**ime and **E**fforts equal **A**dding **M**ore to your life. Once you've figured out who will bring you positive energy 24–7 then you can determine who should be on your team. Just because the person is not energetic does not mean they can't be on your team. Everyone can't be the same to you all the time. You are going to have some people on your team who are not always in sync with you, your dream, and your ideas, but that does not mean they shouldn't be on your team because everyone brings their own qualities to your team, sometimes it can be good and other times it can be bad.

Once I learned in a church sermon that if you want to excel, you have to put yourself in an environment that will help you grow. That can be in an environment where everyone is different but equally yoked for the final goal. Believe me, this will allow you to grow to your potential as a team! One way to determine who is really on your team and will help you grow is by finding a group of people who can teach you something new every day. You want to make sure whomever you choose to hang around (whether it's your competitors, teachers and or inspirers in your field of interest); can help you grow in some shape or form. This is not to say that you need to avoid those who are not in this specific circle of people, because those other individuals can become a great asset to your learning process and growth too, just in a different way! Even more different than being just another person on the team with a different skill!

In other words, I am saying that when you determine who is on your team and that's all you associate yourself with, you experience a difference that allows your true learning potential to take blaze.

Aside from that, determining who is on your team is not just about finding an energetic person to keep you smiling and your coffee warm, but also learning whom you can and cannot trust. Your team needs to include those around you that will be truthful and valuable to your growth process. Think about it, if you are consumed with an unworthy member you are not going to be able to focus on growth. That one person will always be a weak link and invaluable loop whole to your success.

So, my suggestion to you is that when you are determining who you can trust on your journey to success, make sure they believe in your abilities and goals, and everyone is on the same page at all times. One last step in determining who is on your team has to deal with you as an individual and your belief system. Always make sure you believe in yourself in the process because it will only help you determine what person is a good fit for your team.

Lastly, when you are ready to determine who is on your team, ask yourself this question below:

1) Is there anyone currently on my team that represents the word **T.E.A.M.** (People who put in **T**ime and **E**ffort when needed and **A**dd **M**ore when it is not needed)?

_____

_____

_____

Chapter 12
You Can't Make It With Negative Peers

You cannot make it with negative peers, point blank, period end of story! The word "negative" brings a negative or unpleasant connotation and confrontation to many peoples' ears, and for so many different reasons. One reason is because the word "negative" is defined as "expressing denial or disapproval; not positive" (Merriam-Webster, 2012). Why would anyone feel different about this word, based on this definition? When you are on a power trip to success, you want to avoid negativity like you would an oncoming car that wants to knock you off your feet. Negativity will find you regardless of the direction you choose to go in. Negativity can be hidden by a close friend or relative for many years until you make it or become successful. You have to be cautious of when or where negativity displays itself.

Your goal and focus can be thrown off by those who are on a different power trip, trying to take your place. They may go as far as making every attempt they can to be you. You have to be careful of those who don't hold your best interest because they are the ones who will bring you the most negativity. You can always tell because they are always thinking and saying the opposite of what you are thinking and saying. I mean everything they say will be related to something negative. For example, I once had an associate that I normally got scared to share new and old information with because the first words she uttered were always related to something negative that I had already considered and dismissed because I was trying to be positive about the situation. I mean everything she would say would be related to the negative side of the situation. By any means, I am not saying that getting the negative perspective of things from a friend is not good for us, because it can be very helpful to our learning process. However, when someone is constantly expressing the negative side of a situation before considering the positive side of the situation, you can do without it!

When you give advice to a friend or relative, you never, and I mean never try to start off with your negative perspective first. I feel like it goes against showing your support for someone who is in need, especially when it is obvious that the person reached out for positive moral support. I believe encouraging words should always be first when giving a peer or friend advice; definitely prior to giving them the flip view of things. So when I am receiving information I prefer to hear positive things because it symbolizes the first sign of support from a friend, just as I prefer to do when I am giving supportive information to a friend.

So, my suggestion to you is that when you are looking to share your story for moral support to a friend, cousin, or neighbor, think like a detective and investigate any signs of negativity, when advice seems shaky or suspicious. Once you have excluded all the negativity from your circle, you can then move toward a higher step: building positive energy around you.

Here is an extra tip: Think of getting rid of your negative friends like you're throwing out old junk. You know when you are placed in a position where you are forced to get rid of old stuff that you can no longer use. In Ellen DeGeneres's new book *Seriously I'm Kidding,* she stated, "When you're packing up a house, you're forced to decide what you really need verses what you can get rid of" (2011, p. 14). This should be the same method one takes to let go of negative peers, especially when you are trying to keep positive peers in your circle. You need to keep around only those who will have a positive impact on your success; anyone else should be packed up and moved out of your space and territory for life.

To begin this process, ask yourself this question below:

1) Are there negative people in my immediate circle that should be packed up and moved out of my space and territory for life?

_____

_____

Chapter 13
Build Positive Energy Around Yourself

You ever hear that saying, "Hang with only those you want to be associated with"? Well you may also know that other saying: "Those that you hang around represent you." Which would you prefer to be known as in your life?

Let me break it down for you. The difference between the two is simple. In order to make a positive name for yourself, you can either hang with those who are equivalent to where you are currently or where you want to be in life. Or you can hang with those who have already made a negative name for themselves and would enjoy the opportunity to fill your life with that negativity. Before you answer, keep in mind that negativity is only overrated excitement better known as excessive drama. Whereas when you make a positive name for yourself, you drive the overrated excitement in a positive direction. So you have to honestly ask yourself, "Do I want to hang around others that already have a name for themselves or do I want my name to change the success game?"

You have to understand that if you want to be successful, anyone outside of my definition of **P.O.S.I.T.I.V.E.** (**P**eople who **O**ffer **S**uccess, **I**ntellect, **T**enacious **I**nformation, and a **V**ision with no **E**xceptions) is not where you are mentally.

Now that you have had time to understand that, you need to begin thinking about how to build positive energy around you at all times. This chapter is dear to me because I built my life coaching business around the word energy. Energy is defined as "power for working or acting; vigor; strength; and vitality" (Merriam-Webster, 2012). Your success is determined by the type of energy you put into it. It is so important to focus on putting positive energy into your life so that the outcomes of your success can speak for itself.

Building positive energy around yourself first starts with changing your views and outlook on some personal things. If you consider yourself a negative person and you want to build positive energy around yourself, then you may need some additional materials on learning how to be positive. Right now, I can only give you some direction on how to begin the process. That may start with transforming your attitude into positive thinking. I believe the power of thinking positive is deeper than you and I. It is a state that brings contentment and rich filled desires. If you think positive about the vision of your journey, then your greatest desires are fulfilled because you know you will eventually get there. If you plan and expect it, it shall happen!

Building positive energy can also include choosing specific foods, a specific workout regimen, and/or basically just learning how to be positive yourself.

Building positive energy is also about finding balance. It's alright to have your down days and your unmotivated times in life, but that is only okay if you can bounce back from it. One way to do that is by surrounding yourself with positive and energetic family members, friends, and co-workers. As you read on the first page of this chapter, I also associate building energy around yourself with the type of company you keep in your space. While listening to an interview with Taraji P. Henson on the Wendy Williams Show, I overheard Taraji say that her dad once told her "You have to stop hanging around those who have the same problem as you and get with those that have the solution." Like many other quotes, this one stood out for me, because 1) Taraji P. Henson is from my home town and like I, she also represents what it takes to overcome your past to make success your future; and 2) this is a huge step in learning how to build positive energy around yourself as well as learning to use your resources (Discussed in Chapter 9 of this book).

I believe that positive energy builds strength. This is why I chose this as my company slogan. It's a reminder to me and my clients that positive energy is very important to our growth as individuals and as a team. With that in mind, building positive energy could also be included in your daily repertoire through your own personal slogan, quote, motto, or resolution, as well as those that you hear by someone else that relate more to your life than those presented in this book.

So, my suggestion to you is that you think about those you spend time with and determine who is bringing positive energy and who is not. Positive energy should be a long-term goal because it will keep your attitude in check and positive people around you.

Lastly, after reading the last chapter and having time to determine who the negative people were in your immediate circle, you should be able to now ask yourself these questions below:

1) How can I be sure that everyone I have chosen to keep in my new immediate circle will make a positive impact on my success?

   _____

   _____

   _____

2) What positive skills will each individual contribute to my success?

   _____

   _____

   _____

Chapter 14
Build Credibility With Others Along The Way

When you go after what you want in life, you have to go after it with the right people. Now that you have completed the last two activities in Chapter 12 and 13, you should have a better understanding that this means finding people who are in your area of interest that will have an impact on your overall success. You want to find established and already accomplished individuals who you can build rapport and exchange ideas with. Oprah stated in her biography written by Kathy Kelley and titled *Oprah* (2010) that "No one makes it alone (...) everyone who has achieved any level of success in life was able to do so because something or someone served as a beacon to light the way" (p. 575). You want to find that one person who can lead you in the direction your heart intends to go in, someone who can ultimately serve as a beacon in your life and lights the way to your future.

This starts with learning how to build credibility with others. When you exchange ideas with others, this allows you to shed light on them; what they may or may not know about you, and how your skills and abilities can contribute to the current field prior to speaking with you. Another good reason for building credibility with others in your field of interest is to share your unique and or common interest; for example, begin building rapport with a company founder in the area you want to be part of.

Another great way to build your credibility with others is by preparing to speak about yourself and your assets. I think of this as your verbal business card. This is where an opportunity can present itself! In another example, if a person likes what you are saying and they see that what you are saying is different from what has already been presented to them, they will begin to see how they can use your skills. They may feel that their already-established company or business has been missing is you and your brilliant, unique, and clever ideas. This is why it is important to have your verbal business card ready for presentation every second of your life! Just think: if you did not have it ready and you ran into the highest paid person in your industry at the airport and he/she asked you what you would like to do for a living, you'd be stuck!

One way to build credibility with others is to give credit back to others who have already supported you thus far. If there is someone else who is responsible for serving as a beacon in your life and they have either been helping you along your journey or paid the price for you to get where you are today, you need to give them credit for the part they played in your life. That may be to GOD first (or whomever you praise as your Almighty), then a relative, friend, sponsor, and or mentor, but whoever it is, you need to honor them for your success. Even if it has been short-term success, you have to give credit when and where it is due. Just as I have done in this book with honoring those who have shared life quotes that stood out for me during my journey.

Giving credit where it is due will only help you in the long run. For example, when you give credit to others, they will want to help you more because that rapport and trust has been built, especially when you have taken the time to show them your appreciation for their part in your success. No matter how big you get in life, you want to always recognize those who have helped you make a difference in your life. In the end, these are the individuals you want to say you can trust, depend on, and want to keep on your team on a long-term basis. This is one way to build credibility with others who have been a great support system for you. You can also give back to others in the community by volunteering your time or offering motivational speaking to those who have not made it as far as you have. This has been a great way for me to build creditability with so many people within my community.

Monique Hicks mentioned in a *JET Magazine* Interview (April 4, 2010) awhile back "Being a good human being is what validates you" (p. 28). I feel that when you are genuinely good to others and you give freely back to the world, it makes you stand out from others. No matter how much you accomplish and how you look at the work you put in to build your brand in society, there is always something that should keep you grounded in believing that it is important to give back to others. That can be anyone of your choice, a homeless shelter, family member, friend, nonprofit organization, regardless, you have to give back and this is also what it means to give credit when it is due to others. If you have something that God has blessed you with, be it talent or something else, you have to serve it to others at some point in your life. God never give us dreams, journeys, and talents to keep for ourselves. Can you imagine not being able to share any of your experiences with a friend? What would be the reason you would be holding everything in?

Think of giving back like that! There is no way you can go on in life, gaining, and not sharing! In the Bible, it states under Romans 12:6 "In his grace, God has given us different gifts for doing certain things well. So if God has given you the ability to prophesy, speak out with as much faith as God has given you. If your gift is serving others, serve them well; if you are a teacher, teach well; if your gift is to encourage others, be everything; if it is giving, give generously; if God has given you leadership ability, take the responsibility seriously. And if you have a gift for showing kindness to others, do it gladly" (Holy Bible, New Living Translation, 2004, page 866). I say whatever it is that you are good at, build off it, and share it with others in order to become one with God. Becoming one with God, can also bring you more success than you could ever imagine! I will not go any further in explaining this in the spiritual sense because this is not the time, place nor book for this but I did want to give a spiritual perspective for the believers (in Jesus Christ) that are reading this book.

Building credibility with others is also about planning for those you would like to meet that you feel may be interested in helping you build credibility. As an entrepreneur, you will want to plan to meet people who can make things happen in your life. That can start with making a list of those you would like to network with in your future career.

In order to build credibility and rapport that leaves an impression on another person, you also have to "Dress the Part." When the time comes, you will want to always make sure you are professionally presentable. You want to be clean from head to toe and have that million-dollar look. You know that look where you look like you make a million dollars but really you do not? You ever heard of that saying, "your presentation is everything"? That is exactly what you want to be thinking about when you are dressed professionally and trying to build credibility.

You remember when growing up, you could tell the difference between a real cop and a mall cop. Something about the mall cops didn't put any fear in your heart, but if a real cop came knocking on your door, you'd get nervous. It's almost the same fear you get as an adult when a cop gets behind you when you're driving and puts his lights on. The stance of a cop can be just nerve-wracking. Something about the way they stand at your window with one hand on their gun holster while they are pointing the other hand at you asking you for your license and registration. The look they give behind their shades makes you feel guilty right away! My point is that it's all about presentation!

The same scenario goes for military personnel. Their look and uniform alone demands respect. Growing up I had uncles who were in the military, but one in particular that I admired as a kid, was a second lieutenant at the Washington, DC Army National Guard. I remember going over there a lot as a kid and I just felt protected by being in the presence of his employees and him at that time. Even the women were great to be around! Whenever he had his army gear on at our family functions, I would get overjoyed because I was a member of his family. I really enjoyed being his niece during that time! My dad was also a military man in the Marines when I was very young and just looking at his picture as an adult brings chills to my body. My father's picture in that marine's uniform still speaks diligence, power, leadership, success, and honorable representation. I have always been proud to be his daughter as well!

When you are looking to make an impression on others, you should be the first to evaluate your look in order to determine if you have the look that fits who you are supposed to be in a professional sense. Steve Harvey mentioned in one of his books, *Straight Talk, No Chaser* (2010), that if you have the look that screams "My face, my body, and my clothes are nothing special—completely unworthy of anyone's time and attention, even my own" (p. 110), then you cannot expect anyone else to devote any time and attention to you. In the same chapter, Steve Harvey also stated that you should be able to make a statement that says, "I really like me, and you should know by looking at me that I do" (p. 110). These are the thoughts you want to have in your head when you are looking to make a fashion statement in a person's presence.

Keep in mind that building credibility with others can also start with socially networking with others in the area where you would like to be associated.

So, my suggestion to you is to always represent yourself professionally, knowledgeably, fearlessly, and confidently in who you are and where you want to be in life. Also, remember: you are what you wear, how you speak, and how you look! If your look speaks success, then that's where you will be! Rev Run stated in his book titled *Words of Wisdom: Daily Affirmations of Faith from Run's House to Yours,* "you will get where you are going a lot faster if you look like you're already there. So dress and think as if you are the right person for the job" (2008, p. 2). I believe this is so important when you are making strides to the top!

Also remember that by doing this, it will show those who are already established and accomplished in your area of interest what they have been missing in their business.

Let's not forget that building credibility can also start with giving back to others who have supported you along the way. In general, giving back is important to your growth and success. I always believed that in order to get something, you have to give something! As the great Reverend Run also said in his book mentioned earlier (*Words of Wisdom: Daily Affirmations of Faith from Run's House to Yours*), "you must learn how to give before you can receive" (2008, p. 1). This means that until you understand what it means to give back, you cannot expect to receive. Again, when you give without any expectations, you get more than you ever expected in return.

Lastly, ask yourself this question below:

1) Am I taking the right and appropriate measures to build credibility with others in my current industry?

_____

_____

_____

Chapter 15
Prepare For Change Before It Comes

One of the best ways to life coach yourself into success is learning how to prepare for unexpected and expected change. You want to always expect change in your life because without change there is no progress, no future, and no growth. Sometimes when we are working toward our goals, we have some kind of sense that change will occur. The fact that you are reading this book shows that you are looking for a change.

Although change can be difficult for me because of how quickly it can happen in my life sometimes, I find myself overcoming it by adopting and adjusting as quickly as the change allows me to. So, I want you to understand that change does not always have to be related to a downward spiral. Nelly recently said in an interview with Jamie Foster Brown (*Sister 2 Sister,* 2011) "Some people when they think of change they think negative." Most times people think that when they prepare for change it has to be bad.

For example, I myself cannot handle quick change in careers, especially when I have been used to working the same job routine for over a year. When I used to work full-time with a company that made changes every three to six months, I lost focus along the way. I could not understand how a company that wants you to grow and excel in your current position gives you a change in responsibility more times than you can count on one hand in less than a year. I often asked myself during that time, how can I actually learn from such a position, company, or organization? Now, some people say changes that are made consistently are what promote growth. That may be true, but ask yourself, how can you grow in one position that is supposed to allow you to progress to the next level if the changes keep happening before you finish growing in that one position? I believe that Americans have the hardest time accepting change because change is such a very sensitive topic in America and because we have the freedom to change when we are ready, rather than when someone tells us to.

My take is that in order for someone to grow into their full potential in any given position they need to spend more time where they are before moving to the next level. Sometimes change can come from anywhere and catch you from the blind side. Oftentimes there are people who will throw salt into your game so that you can't recognize the change. Be cautious of those individuals because they are the ones trying to take your spot by blinding you with change you didn't see coming.

So, my suggestion to you is that in order for you to prepare for change, you must first change at your own pace, regardless if it is slow or fast. Take time to understand change and remember to expect it. If you can do that, then you can welcome it into your life. Welcoming change can be a way to overcome your struggles with making changes in general. Just remember that if you can train yourself mentally to prepare for change prior to expecting it then you will always be ahead of the game, especially if you do not know when it is coming!

Lastly, ask yourself this question below:

1) What precautions am I taking in my life to prepare for any unexpected changes that may occur at any moment?

_____

_____

_____

Chapter 16
Let Go Of What You Can't Change

Why do we allow forever to go by before we want to let go of the things we have never been able to change? I know from many meetings with my clients that the phrase "letting go," is hard to do. But, I often ask myself these questions when I think of how hard it is, in general, for anyone to let go of the things we cannot change: Why do we wait until a drastic change takes place in our life and the desire to fix it is out of our reach before we consider letting go? Why do we tend to stress ourselves over things we cannot change? As creatures of habit, we become so fixated on taking matters into our own hands, even when we know we aren't capable of making something change. The truth is that the harder the challenge becomes the more we, as a society, try to control the things we cannot change.

In chapter 7, we discussed how it's important to understand that failing is only the beginning to a new start. Sometimes we have a hard time letting go when we have failed at something. We struggle with letting go even when we realize that the results of the failed experience are out of our control. Shirley Strawberry quoted in her book titled *Strawberry Letter,* "When you fail, practice the art of forgiveness. When you can forgive yourself, you allow yourself to let go of the past. This can sometimes be harder than forgiving others" (2011, p. 101). Shirley learned how to forgive herself by her experiences during her relationships and lifetime.

To be successful at anything we want to do in life, we have to let go of the desire to change things that are out of our control. One reason is because it shifts our focus from what is really important in life. When we focus on things that do not have any relevance to the more important things in our life, it becomes wasted energy.

In Oprah's biography, written by Kitty Kelley and titled *Oprah,* Oprah quoted, "If you concentrate on what you have, you'll end up having more. If you constantly focus on what you don't have, you'll end up having less" (Kelley, p. 545). When we go through trials and tribulations in life we take days to heal but years to let go. What's even worse is that we allow our past to haunt our future. We can't ask for success to take place in our lives and prepare for disaster. That is what you are doing when you allow your past to hinder your future. It's almost like doing a 360-degree turn: starting off with a disaster and ending with a disaster. If something from your past is hanging over your head, you have to let it go for that success you want to come. You really have to consider letting go of your past to embrace your future; this is how we begin to let go of the things we cannot change in our lives. We all go through ups and downs. I truly believe that it is what makes a person appreciate life more. In order to be something, you have to go through something. No one lives a perfect life; at least I have not seen anyone yet in my lifetime! Your past is what it is! In the future you are going to look back and say, "What I been through was worth going through in order to get where I am today." That is how I look at the cards I have been dealt; I have accepted them and learned how to move beyond them in order to have a better future for myself and my family.

I want to shift gears for a minute just to be real with you. I want to share with you how this was one of the last and the hardest chapters even for me to write and I think it's because learning how to let go of things I couldn't change used to be one of the hardest things for me to do in my life. I could probably write an entire book on learning to let go and accept change!

There was a time when I used to live my life pleasing others or sacrificing my peace and sanity for others; I would never let go of anything that happened. I was the person trying to save everyone, and it took me a very long time to realize that a lot of the things that were happening to others were things that I could not change. The things that others were going through were because of the decisions those people made, not mines, but I could not understand that for a very long time. I almost wanted to change the title of this chapter because talking about change can be uncomfortable for me sometimes. However, I could not allow myself to write only about things that make me comfortable in life just to save face from my readers. That would not be fair to you as my readers and supporters. As a writer, it is important for me to write my true experiences because I am a walking testimony and what I have learned from those experiences can help another individual. The more books I write, the more I plan to share about my life experiences until it makes a difference in more than just one person's life.

You know, sometimes the most memorable and cutest quotes come from the most random places! The other day my nail technician, Tim, was talking to me about being happy in life and he said that "sometimes it's not about the money, it's about being happy" and he was right. Most of that happiness starts with letting go of the things you can't change!

Also, as a society, we often have a hard time letting go of how others react to our pending success. While we are on the path to succeed, we encounter unexpected reactions from those we choose to share our experiences with along the way. Sometimes we even go so far as to allow others' actions and attitudes to determine our success. Another person's attitude and actions will never change because of how you approach them. If they were negative before, they will still be negative after you share your good news. Let me say this again: if you encounter someone who is currently negative in your life, remember if they are negative today, they will be negative tomorrow until they are ready to make a change themselves. It may be more than just what you see appear on the outside, it can go farther than you ever considered, like having an off chromosome in their genes that affects their decision making process or how they accept and let go of change. So let it go!

Always keep in mind that when you decide to share good news with people of this nature you will have to accept the reality and accepting this will make it easier to let go of it. It's just one of those things in life we cannot change. For example, I feel that some people with whom I shared my desire to be an author with could really care less. It sounds funny, but I am serious! For the most part everyone in my immediate circle of family and close friends are supportive (hence to get where I am today, I had to limit my circle to only those who were genuinely supportive) but there are still a few haters amongst the bunch (some who are even family). I'm talking about people who can care less if you walk into their presence or not, not to mention write a book! This type of person is very similar to the same type of negative person I will discuss in the next chapter. Let me warn you, just because you let go of them does not mean they will go away.

The haters will read your book and give you all negative feedback and you will respond, "WHAT, BUT HOW?" They will have you all twisted up and tongue tied because you don't know how they could come to such a conclusion when you know there are others already interested in what you have to offer the world. In fact, you may have already established relationships with other authors who want to endorse the same book you are sharing with them. So, learn how to deal with these situations. This can be another step in the right direction of learning how to let go of what you cannot change in life.

You have to be careful of a person with this type of M.O. (mode of operation), especially since you know you can't change any of their reactions toward you. These types of individuals will have you making changes that don't need to be made when really they are dealing with the fact that you have a book/life/career/ family and they don't. They cannot relate to the certain level of success you have reached in your life. So they even share with others, the minute you leave them (basically behind your back), that the gesture of sharing your book with them was only another "ALL ABOUT ME" session. You know why? Sometimes people will never understand your excitement until you became an icon, paid a pretty nickel to share your thoughts! Guess what? Those same individuals (haters) will be back to hear you out!

After going through this situation and many others, I have come to the realization that there's nothing you can do about people with this mentality because they will never have your best interest in mind. They become so good at acting like they are supportive, you don't really know how they really feel until your success begins. I have actually become very good at weeding out the haters from my circle, and let me tell you, it is no easy task! I have learned that the more haters I have, the more focused I become. The more drama they create for me, the more I am blessed! All because I have let go of the things I could not change about what others say and do in their lives.

You should never let the "fake friends" thing get to you because they are who they are from the minute you meet them until the day you realize they are not your real friends. Part of letting go of things you cannot change is learning how to let go of those that are not supportive. If you don't do this, then it will be as sweet as pie to them because you will have let their reaction affect your success!

My suggestion to you is that you need to let go of people who are sewing bad seeds in your life. Seeds that do not help you to grow should not be planted into your future. The same goes for money. For example, if you are a person who is holding tainted money from your past, don't expect to produce pure millions. Life and success doesn't work that way! If you want good, then let go of the bad. When money, people and unimportant things come into your life for the wrong reasons you need to immediately let go of them!

People always ask me why I would never move back home to DC where I was born and raised and continue to represent, but what people don't know is that while I love visiting home, it is always more work than I anticipate. I am always pulled in so many directions by everyone. On top of that I always need an agenda because there are so many people that I just have to see when I am there. I recently joked with a good friend and colleague that I have to always figure out how to see 200 people in 2 days. I am not trying to sound conceited in a way that people just love me, but I am saying it can be stressful sometimes and hard for me to let go of the guilt I feel when I run out of time and I still haven't seen this family member or that friend. I always feel obligated to do so much that oftentimes in this case I don't always know how to weed out the most important tasks.

Truth is, I never know how to let go of the unimportant things in my life. I was raised to accept everyone and every task in my life as important but I learned fast as an adult that there are some unimportant people and things that should be avoided. By unimportant, I mean people and things that can hinder your success and do not have valuable meaning in your life. Generally speaking, whenever I traveled home I didn't know how to let go of all the things in my life that were not the most important to my health and success. However, after a few disappointments, I caught on pretty fast. If I didn't catch on when I did, most of these unimportant things would have led me to failure. Sunday Adelaja stated in his book *Money Won't Make You Rich* that "success is on the other side of failure, so have courage to move forward" (p. 21). You have to let go in order to move forward, and you have to move forward in order to get beyond the drama you are dealing with in your life right now. As I stated earlier, letting go is no easy task at all, but it is necessary if you want happiness. Remember you cannot get what is coming to you if you don't let go of those things you have no control over. Learn to let go of all the things you cannot change! This is a huge step to succeeding in life!

Lastly, ask yourself this question below:

1) What are some of the things in my life that I cannot change and need to let go in order for me to become successful?

_____
_____
_____

Chapter 17
Plan Your Goals

Planning is so important in making something come to life. If you believe in something, you have to plan it out. You should avoid planning just to plan, but rather you have to plan it correctly. In other words, you should try to plan your goals and make daily progress toward accomplishing them. Planning correctly means taking time to put mental images of your dream together into one picture, so that you may see everything from top to bottom, and the beginning to end! Once you have a vision (full picture) of your goals and you have begun taking steps toward setting those goals in place, you will be able to plan for those goals accordingly. Also when you have a full picture of your goals mentally played out, you will also have a complete visual sense of where you want to be in life.

While I believe in opportunities, first and second chances, and luck, there are some who also believe that planning is still an important process to a success future. I read in a New York Article on Wendy Williams that nothing in her life has happened by chance and she quoted "Virtually everything in my life I have plotted on to get it, nothing has happened by fluke" (Fishman, 2005). In other words, all the success you see her enjoying now, as a current Daytime TV host and a past radio jockette, she has earned it because she planned for it. In the same article, it was mentioned by her best friend Lisa Carnegie that Wendy always had a "futuristic vision" which Lisa states is "an ability to plot the future, her future. She was the girl who walked around with a to-do list and a plan. If you asked her twenty years ago what was her twenty-year plan, she had it" (Fishman, 2005).

I cannot stress to you how important planning is in life. Anything you would like to achieve needs to be planned out all the way down to the time of day, month, and year you would like to see those goals take place. This starts by writing out your steps. Planning brings better preparation for all the mishaps, as well as the good we may or may not expect to take place in our lives. Planning puts our thoughts in a better mental space because it helps us see the whole picture. Without planning, so many things can go wrong! When we don't plan, we don't give ourselves a chance to see the whole picture. Seeing the whole picture allows us to see all the problems before they occur. Seeing the whole picture also allows us to see all the great things to look forward to making our dream come true.

Planning has done wonders for me over the years. To this day, I plan everything out, including when and where I want to live even if it does not take place. I planned out how far I wanted to further my education. I planned where I felt I needed to live in order to be successful (hence my very recent move from Miami to Los Angeles), and the type of living expenses it would take to fulfill that dream. Even if what you plan does not take place in the way you see it, you still have to pat yourself on the back for planning. For me, when things don't go how I planned them, I still feel like a winner because I was ahead of the game with my thoughts about where I wanted to be in the future. It doesn't matter that they didn't take place or add up to how I originally planned them, but the fact that I planned them gave me some idea of where things might have went wrong; and believe me, there will be some things that will go wrong!

While planning is a very good method I have found for succeeding in life, as mentioned above, not only will there be times when your reality deviates from the original plan, there will also be other times when what you did not plan will take place. For example, years ago when I was in grad school, I found myself planning the age I wanted to get married, but six years after that age, I was still not married. To be very honest with you, it was not because I did not want to get married or did not have the mate to do so; it was simply because I had not taken the time to plan it out completely. I didn't want to because it just wasn't as much of a priority as it was to accomplish my goals like finishing school, becoming a doctor, life coach, and author. I had heard from previous married couples the energy and time it took to plan a wedding and I was just not interested in planning one. So prior to the year 2011 (six years after the age I had originally planned to get married), I still had not dedicated any serious planning toward making my dream wedding come true.

Fast forward a year now, and I am very happy to report that I did have the wedding of my dreams in 2011 with a beautiful backdrop on the rooftop at a very luxurious Miami Hotel. It's all because I finally took the energy and time to plan my dream wedding correctly. I truly believe that without the proper planning, it would not have been as beautiful as I dreamed it to be. This is also due to my awesome wedding planner, Tessie Watts, and her Twin Creations Team of West Palm Beach, and a whole entourage of others who all did a good job at making my day extra special, even with all the things we did not plan taking place on that day!

So, remember that when you make plans to go after that dream job or come up with the perfect budget plan to get that dream house, it can only happen the way you dreamed of it to be if you plan it ahead of time. Here is a lesson, when things deviate from your original plan: Do not let it ruin your motivation. Instead double plan, so that you will always have a back-up plan.

In addition, when things start happening in your life that you did not plan to take place, you will have to react fast, because in most cases you may be given little or no time to prepare or plan for that change. How can you, if it has already happened? Now keep in mind too that just because you didn't plan for something to happen does not mean you are stuck or cannot overcome the situation.

Let me share a lesson I learned from situations like this in my past. Growing up in my early to mid-twenties, I never planned when I wanted to have a child. I always felt if it happened, I would deal with the situation then, because then I would know it would be in God's plan for my life. In fact, at one point in my life, when I was furthering my graduate studies, I was positive I didn't want children. As the oldest of eight, something about that experience changed my outlook on having children. But as fate would have it, in 2006, almost seven years ago now, I found out I was pregnant. I didn't know what I was going to do because it wasn't planned and it definitely was not in my plans for "my" near future.

When I had more time to think about it, I became affected by what others might say since I was in grad school. I could hear my family's and friends' opinionated voices in my head saying "Not miss plan it all." Lucky for me, a few days earlier, I had just passed my master's thesis oral defense and that meant I was done with my master's program. So I felt like I was at a place where I could stop school if I wanted to, but I didn't because at the time it wasn't in my plans. So, even with a newborn baby, I went on to begin my doctorate program in Counseling Psychology and with proper planning, I was also able to complete a huge portion of my doctorate program after my son was born.

Let me sidetrack you for a minute, the labor pains were not something I prepared myself for mentally and I don't think I would have been able to do so, since I had never experienced it before. However, I will say that aside from the double labor I experienced, the C-section, the two epidurals, and the 36 hours of attempting to give birth, having my son became one of the best unplanned experiences of my life.

As a mother, when you experience giving another human being life, even if it may not be in your plans anytime soon, remember that planning your life and your children's life can be a motivator to learning how to plan effectively in general. In addition, you can learn how to prioritize their planning accordingly if you remember this important step when you are life coaching yourself.

Although the birth of my son was unplanned, I got into action mode and began planning very quickly. I felt I would be going against everything I stood for if I had a child and didn't plan his life out, too. I had people to tell, dates to consider, further education plans to think about, and baby items that needed to be purchased. Above it all, I continued my life as I had originally planned it prior, and worked my newborn baby into those plans.

So, my suggestion to you is that you never let anything stop you from chasing your dreams, not even your children. I know it is not this simple for everyone's case and I will agree that when you make the decision to have a child or children, birthing and raising them can slow you down, but it also puts you in a place where you gain patience, understanding, and definitely good practice for planning. Remember, while it is your decision to have children, you may get slowed down a bit, but their existence will not cause you to fail.

Planning helps you to deal with the unforeseen. So, next time something happens in your life that you did not plan, remember to get into action and begin planning as much you can, until you can't plan anymore. You will know when you begin to over-plan. For example, have you ever planned something twice and forgot that you planned it the first time around? That is so me, and that is when you know you have over-planned for yourself! Remember, try to see the whole picture of what your life would be like after you coach yourself into what you want: plan for the expected and the unexpected because you never know what is coming your way!

Lastly, ask yourself this question below:

1) What steps do I need to take in order to plan my goals effectively so that they come to life?

_____

_____

_____

Chapter 18
Set Real Life Goals

When you are passionate about something in life, setting goals to get there should be easy. If you know what you really want to do, or know where you really want to be in life, then planning to get there should come with great desire. How many times have you thought about something you wanted to do but did not make any plans or set any goals to get there? This often happens because you lack the desire to put your mind in the right place to get there. Other times, people lack the motivation to make goals because of money concerns. People sometimes allow their lack of money to get in the way of setting real goals for themselves. What people with this mentality don't realize is that setting real goals starts free with a cheap three-ring spiral notebook and an ink pen. Or even a pencil if that is what you like to use! Whatever it takes! You don't even have to begin jotting down your plans on a computer right away. You can take baby steps and start somewhere (as I often hear my in-laws say). When some of the richest people in the world saw a vision for themselves, do you think they just started blurting out their plans to everyone? Absolutely not! Since riches come with careful thinking and planning, I can bet you any amount of money they didn't! Instead they began setting their goals on paper.

Goal setting does not have to be as complicated as one may make it. You have to know what it is that your heart desires, what you are passionate about and what is important to you? In order to get the answer to this question, you first need to understand what life is about in general, know your purpose in life (know what it is you were placed on Earth to do—as discussed in Chapter 4). You also have to know your mission in life, and that means figuring out what you are inspired to do in this lifetime. Part of growing is understanding the next direction you are destined to go in. That begins with writing things down that you believe in and want to see happen. This is how setting real goals begins. This is also where you determine what goals need to be realistically set in your life.

In Dr. Ian Smith's book titled *The 4 Day Diet*, he suggests that one can use the **S.M.A.R.T.** Principle for setting realistic goals in their life. The **S.M.A.R.T.** Principle stands for **S**pecific, **M**easurable, **A**ttainable, **R**ealistic, and **T**imeframe. When you are ready to set realistic goals for yourself, you want to make sure you create goals that are **S**pecific (broken down to clarity); **M**easurable (concrete, obtainable and can be monitored through progress); and **A**ttainable (tangible and reachable). As Dr. Ian Smith (2008) wrote, this goal should require hard work and true dedication, otherwise it may mean you are not pushing yourself enough and may be setting the bar too low for a goal. The next one on the list, **R**ealistic, means to make your goals very concrete to accomplish. The last one on the list was **T**imeframe, which means that your goals can be completed through timed intervals or in a timed sequence. Dr. Ian Smith stated that one's goal should be linked to a time clock in order to keep focus in the right direction. With the **S.M.A.R.T.** Principle you can become creative in setting your goals realistically to your comfort and lifestyle.

Now that we've discussed how you should set your goals, let's go over where you should begin setting your goals. First, I would encourage you to learn from yourself, what it is in life that makes your heart beat. For example, try to think of who you are at the real core of your existence. Second, determine where your passion lies in leading you toward your success. For example, I took my brother down to his school orientation a year ago at Full Sail University in Orlando, and while I was there, I was reading a Degree Guide Pamphlet that defined success in a way that was quite simple but powerful to me. The pamphlet stated that every person has a different way of defining success. I took that definition in and pondered its meaning throughout the entire 3-hour orientation. By the way, Full Sail is the real deal for anyone who is interested in getting an education in music, marketing, production, television and movies (Platinum Creative, 2011), but the definition was so profound to me that I felt like I understood something else beyond those words.

One thing that came to mind was how we can take the definition of success and apply it to our lives based on how we see others succeed. Even worse, we judge our own success from the material things we see others with in their lives. As humans, we get accustomed to defining our own success by another person's success. Instead we should use another person's successful and unsuccessful life journeys as lessons about what we should and should not do in our own life journey.

There are other times we define success by what society tells us is accepted as success. We allow others to even go as far as defining what success means to us. Then we take it a step further and begin to follow in the footsteps of someone else's ideal lifestyle of success. For me, I find myself often measuring my success by my son's happiness. Sadly, but it is a reality for me, I feel even better about my own success when my husband and other family members are happy with something I have done for them because of my success. Rarely do I ever look at success based on something I have done for myself, unless it is a big purchase and it's evident, even though I define my success by quality and not quantity. For example, when I bought my second Lexus I felt I had done something that was not commonly done by others and for me that was a dose of success. Next, when I defended my dissertation and completed my doctorate, I began to feel an even higher dose of success. However, I feel those things are more of quality than quantity. If I wanted, I could have more of each, but just having one is rewarding, it still holds the same value in my life and is just enough.

In addition to that, publishing my first book, maintaining a blog, running two businesses and working a full-time and part-time job were all the things that I considered myself to be successful at and because I had successfully managed all these things, that's how I measured my success. Now that may not be your typical idea of success or another person's way of defining or measuring success in their lives, but that is how I defined success. However, it did not matter to me how I defined it because I couldn't really measure it until I made someone else happy.

If I could make someone else happy, whether it be a family member or close friend, then I knew I had succeeded in my own life because without that success I would not have the resources to make anyone happy. For some odd reason, my measurement of how successful I was in life was judged by how I made someone else happy, even if it was sharing wisdom, a quick exchange of information, etc. As long as I knew I shared something with someone they didn't know prior to meeting me and they expressed their thanks with a smile, I felt like I had won and I would walk away and say "I DID IT AGAIN"! When you can say that and feel good about it, regardless of what it is you have done, then you have reached some height of success in your life, and you need to THANK GOD for that. You don't have to measure success in the way that I do, but find a way to determine where your life is going, how successful you currently are and have been thus far. Find a way to measure your success based on the results you display every day.

I believe that taking time to define what success means to you will be another step toward setting real life goals for yourself. Also, think about some of the guiding principles or values you are destined to live by, because they will help you determine what direction your goals need to go in. Doing this will also help you determine which goals are realistic for you! The results of setting real goals in your life will give you the same amount of excitement I get from helping others learn things they didn't know prior to meeting me.

So my suggestion to you is that you make goals that you feel are applicable to and for you. Try not to set goals just to say you are setting them or simply to have them. Rather, plan them, set them, and make them real for you. In addition, you should become obsessed with your goals as much as you can. Rev Run recently tweeted, "You will only have SIGNIFICANT success when you're border line obsessed with your goals" (@RevRunWisdom, February 28, 2011 at 6:00 pm Eastern Time). So, remember your goals need to be something you show compulsive concern about, and keep in mind, a goal is not realistic if it's not reachable!

Lastly, ask yourself this question below:

1) After planning my goals, what steps do I still need to take in order to make them come to life?

_____

_____

_____

Chapter 19
Clear The Clutter And Visualize Your Goals

Aside from planning your goals and using the **S.M.A.R.T.** Principle to set your goals, you should also take some time to visualize your goals. My suggestion to you is that you make this the third step after planning and setting your goals. Visualizing your goals allows your thoughts to be played out in your mind before any physical action in planning can take place. The first step in doing this is learning how to clear the clutter of distorted images of any negativity blocking your dream from coming to life.

Some researchers will argue that it takes seven days to create a habit, and others will argue that it takes 72 hours to learn a habit. Whatever the case is, that's not my calling, all I can speak on is my perspective as a life coach. When I have clients who are having trouble with deleting distorted images from their mind; I encourage them to practice removing those distorted images until it becomes a habit. I often tell my clients that changing a behavior can only be done after a person practices it enough that it becomes familiar to them. Sometimes it can take days and other times it can take weeks, but for the most part, when the motivation to change is present, the practice becomes easier. Before you know it the habit to clear the clutter from your vision is consistent.

Keep in mind that if you want to do something right, you have to practice the routine until it becomes part of your natural routine. Learning how to clear the clutter for your vision is doing just that; practicing it to create a habit.

Another part of clearing the clutter from your vision is learning how to see from a different viewpoint, learning how to see from another part of your brain that produces a different perspective on life. According to Allen Sargent (1999), the purpose of accessing the other mind's eye is to see how we function from both sides of the brain. As a result, accessing this second side of the brain can help a person visualize how and where they want to be in life. Sargent believes that visualization is one of the main tools for making change in your life. If you can allow yourself to remove the clutter, you can experience a more desirable visualization for your life. Sargent (1999) also stated that "visualization is the key to identifying and then getting what you want in your life" and by doing this you can "discover the secret of turning your dreams into reality" (back cover).

Now, when it comes to defining visualization, it is a little bit different from just using the other side of your brain to get a different perspective; it is more like putting action into your vision. Now that means that once you have discovered a different perspective of your vision from the other viewpoint, you are now acknowledging it and you can begin forming a mental picture of it.

According to the *Merriam-Webster Online Dictionary* (2012), to visualize means "to make visible; as; to see or form a mental image of; and to form a mental visual image." That means that when a person has a preconceived thought or idea of something they want to accomplish in their lifetime, they visualize it as a goal, but only after they have acknowledged that thought or idea as a goal.

Sometimes a person can go a lifetime trying to accomplish that preconceived thought or idea, but in most cases he/she hope that it happens sooner than later. One of the reasons it does not always take place sooner is because sometimes goal seekers leave their goal as "a thought" and do not move it into action. In other cases, they are left at the planning stage. What's worse is that sometimes they never take a second look at their original goals again. What people don't understand is that if you can't ever finish one goal, you will never be able to finish twenty goals. It is just not happening! You have to find discipline within yourself to see your goals through, once you plan them. I never understood how people could make huge goals for themselves and express so much interest in their goals, shouting out to the world how they want something so badly, but then they don't follow through in accomplishing the goal. It's almost like going to the grocery store and not buying anything, so why go?

In order to see your vision through, you cannot continue to go after something in life, make plans toward it, but continue to fail at seeing it through.

It is really hard for me to understand the motivation someone may gain from planning a goal, after they set a deadline to complete a goal, and aside from any substantial life circumstances, they do not put any more interest into seeing it through. From here on out, when we set goals, remember we have to check our laziness at the ticket counter and pick up our luggage of motivation at the baggage claim or else we will continue to fail at clearing the clutter in our mind to see our vision through.

Visualizing your dream is about motivating yourself to make it happen. My point is, when you are ready to take your dream to another level, use whatever method or technique you can to clear the clutter and begin visualizing your dream. For example, you can practice being still and allowing yourself to be in the moment with your thoughts until you can see a visual or feel your dream come to life inside of you. Whatever it takes to see your dream through should be done without any excuses. As mentioned earlier in this chapter, visualizing your dream allows you to play out in your mind what you want to take place in action. This also becomes an opportunity to do a trial run, the same way you would in planning your goals. In your visual you will be able to see the things you don't want to take place and the things you know you want to go after in your lifetime. In addition, you should be able to determine what's missing in your planning; what's reasonable financially and what's more out of your reach when it comes to attaining your goals. Forming a mental picture of the goals you would like to achieve can be beneficial for you as the believer because it will encourage you to make it happen.

So, my suggestion to you is that you don't have to be afraid to live your dream out in your mind. Visualizing your dream can bring a rush of adrenaline like no other, but seeing it through is an even greater feeling of accomplishment.

Remember, even if the goal is one of the hardest to accomplish in your life, you have to do what it takes to see it through, or you will never trust yourself to make future goals. On top of that, it does not mean that you will never want to make any big goals for yourself because you never could accomplish the one big goal you have been running from. So you may continue to set smaller goals for yourself on a longer term than usual because it is safer to do and that alone will not get you where you want to be in life. You have to discipline yourself and prepare to jump over some deep hurdles before you can finish the race to success.

Lastly, ask yourself this question below:

1) What steps have I taken to clear the clutter from my mind that is blocking the perfect vision of my goals?

_____

_____

_____

Chapter 20
Act Today For A Better Tomorrow

Did you know that if you act today, good things will happen for you tomorrow? Once you go through this experience you will never miss another opportunity coming your way. I am a firm believer in never letting an opportunity pass you by, regardless of how big or small your chances may seem. A true example of this took place for me recently.

Before I begin sharing that example, let me say that over the past two to three years I have reached out to so many actors, TV hosts, authors, and high-profile Black magazine editors with the hopes of someone recognizing my talent as a writer. However, like any other aspiring artist or writer, with the push to connect and succeed comes rejection. Yes, I too have experienced that! In fact I have experienced more than my share of this over the past few years. No matter what, I always believed that if I continued to work hard and continued to dedicate myself to my craft and what I love to do, then eventually my success would prevail over the rejection. Let me be the first to say, it worked, because if it didn't, you would not be reading this book right now. I also would not be sharing this as my testimony either!

Now, I have to be honest, there have been times when so many rejections made me reconsider what my true passion really was and how I should make use of it. I began taking some steps back to see if maybe I should tap into one of my other talents/roles/responsibilities/duties and try to make that my craft or art. Clearly, what I learned from that experience is that "YOU CANNOT PUT YOUR PASSION WHERE IT DOES NOT FIT."

In other words, you cannot bring a spark to something that was never supposed to be lit up in the first place. On the flip side, you cannot turn off something that never dies within you. If your heart and passion is with a specific goal or interest, it should never end because of rejection. You just cannot reinvent a passion. It will not work! This is why it is so important to learn what your purpose in life is all about (see Chapter 4 for additional information on this topic) because otherwise you will let things come into your life and derail your focus. Once you learn what your passion and purpose in life is, no one will ever be able to change what lies in your heart. Not even you!

In relating this back to the example and opportunity that recently took place in my life, I recently learned about a very reputable Public Relations Agency in Orlando through online research. I called the agency and for a few weeks we discussed opportunities for hiring them to help me build my personal brand through social media. As a side note, this was something I learned to do when I was checking out my competition and studying where I wanted to be in life.

During one of those calls, I was offered a list of references to check out authors that had used their services in the past and were currently beyond successful. I accepted the offer and eventually the list was emailed to me. Sadly, a few weeks went by and I forgot about the references. Another few weeks went by and I received another call from this agency asking me for an update and if I had decided about hiring them. At that time I began to doubt their services, thinking they really just wanted to get paid because they were so consistent in calling me. Later I realized it really wasn't that, it was an opportunity (knocking at my door several times) that I could not see. During that phone call I kept it professional and honest and told them I had not had the time to think about it and that I was sorry. I also kept it professional for the sake that there was a possibility that I may use them in the future. So after that call, I immediately begin calling the references. I must say I had first time luck in this situation because my first caller was my last. This guy was someone who made me a believer in me and my craft. In fact, he proved to me that hard work does pay off in the end. This guy's name was Jason Jennings of Jennings Solutions, out of San Francisco.

When I called, he answered his phone right away, ready to converse with whomever was on the other end. He had no idea it was me, but the fact that he answered his phone with no expectations is what had me excited to speak with him. You and I both know there are a lot of celebrities and high-profile individuals who do not answer their own phone and will have their assistants give you a call back. Sometimes, you never get the opportunity to speak with them. Later in the conversation, when I was thanking Jason for his time, he told me that normally I would not have been able to reach him at the time that I called. So, I guess that was my luck at that moment and on that day. Might I add, as fate would have it, it was a good moment! You never know when someone will give you the time and day to shine. You never know when it will be your lucky day to share your dream with another who has made theirs come to light. That day was the beginning of new hope for me. When you act, you get results. When you believe, you get your dream. It's that simple.

That day, Jason not only gave me a good reference for that PR Agency, he also gave me information on how to get started and succeed as a speaker and publisher. He even took extra time to answer a few more of my questions. What I like the most about Mr. Jennings (the author of New York Times Bestseller, *Less Is More*, which is the same statement I used earlier in this book, prior to meeting Jason) was that he was patient and he was passionate about helping me. He offered tips and even the use of his own team to help me later on down the line. When he saw how appreciative I was, he told me that from talking on the phone with me, he liked me. In my head, that meant "He respected my approach and ambition to be an author" and it showed when he told me he would write a blurb on the back of this book when it was done. Long story short, we made arrangements to meet the following week at his next speaking engagement in Boca Raton, FL. If you don't believe me when I tell you that acting today helps to get you a better tomorrow, this is my testimony that it does. You have to believe in yourself and your ability to make things happen for you because if you do not, your dreams will always be something of "the tomorrow."

So, my suggestion to you is that you never let an opportunity pass you by because you just don't feel like acting on that opportunity that day. If you can remember reading earlier in this book in Chapter 9 (Utilize Your Resources) where I discussed how I attempted to connect with others in my field, but none of them were open and accepting like Mr. Jennings. Not one of the conversations

I had with the others in my field was like the opportunity I had experienced with Jason overall. I have learned from everyone that I have connected with while writing this book (even if it was a negative response), but after sitting down with Jason and listening to how supportive he was of my future, how excited he was to introduce me to anyone that stopped by while we were talking, how he volunteered to be my mentor and show me how to make it successfully as an author and speak, I genuinely felt like my connection with Jason was different than any other celebrity that I had met. After that experience, I believe this is the start of a new tomorrow for me.

Jason Jennings has no idea how much I was listening to him on the phone that day, and how his words will forever change me. During our phone conversation he stated, "Half of winning is being the last one standing." As a mother, a new wife, writer, author, life coach, and a believer in Christ and in my craft, I plan to be the last winner standing in every race I attempt to run. This is the only way I will stand out from the rest and begin to outshine my peers. This is just where my drive to succeed in life has always been. I don't want to be anyone else besides myself and overcoming being labeled as the average allows me to do that! Moments like this helped me to relate to anyone who has done what it took to overcome their past, and their yesterdays to make tomorrow a successful future!

Believe me readers, if we don't act today, how can we look forward to a better tomorrow? Ask yourself this question and respond below.

1) If we don't act today, how can we look forward to a better tomorrow?

_____

_____

_____

Chapter Activities Worksheet

Chapter 1 What Does Life Mean To You?

1) Life means _____ to me! I know this is true because when I apply _____ to my life, it makes me feel _____.

No one else can define what your life means to you more than you can. Applying that definition to your world on a day-to-day basis will only boost your confidence in knowing what life means to you.

Chapter 2 What Does Life Coaching Yourself Mean?

1) What does life coaching yourself mean to you?

_____

_____

_____

Chapter 3 Do You Trust Yourself?

1) I trust myself to do _____. I know this is true because I never _____ an opportunity when it becomes available to me.

Chapter 4 Know What Your Purpose Is In Life

1) What is My Purpose in Life?

_____

_____

_____

2) Am I going after desirable behaviors that will help me find my purpose in life?

_____

_____

_____

Chapter 5 Dare To Dream But Don't Strive For Another's Dream

1) What is my dream?

_____

_____

_____

2) Is my dream for me because it fulfills me and not anyone else's?

_____

_____

_____

Chapter 6 Think Like A Leader To Become One

1) Are you thinking like a leader when it comes to running and implementing your business goals?

_____

_____

_____

2) Are you taking the right steps to thinking and becoming a leader towards your personal goals?

_____

_____

_____

Chapter 7 Understand Failing Is Only The Beginning

1) What have you learned from your failed experiences that is going to help you move forward?

_____

_____

_____

2) What are the positive steps you are taking to move beyond your failed experiences?

_____

_____

_____

Chapter 8 Check Out Your Competition

1) What is the best way to compete with myself to come out on top every time?

_____

_____

_____

2) How can I check out my competitor in a way that it keeps me focused on succeeding at my ultimate goal?

_____
_____
_____

3) What can I learn from my competitor that will help me to excel in my industry?

_____
_____
_____

Chapter 9 Utilize Your Resources

1) What resources are available to me and how can I use those resources to capitalize on more opportunities that are available for me?

_____
_____
_____

Chapter 10 Understand Others' Purpose In Your Life

1) What is the purpose God has placed each of those individuals into your life?

_____
_____
_____

2) How can this relate to my desire to be successful?

_____
_____
_____

Chapter 11 Determine Who Is On Your Team

1) Is there anyone currently on my team that represents the word **T.E.A.M.** (People who put in Time and Effort when needed and Add More when it is not needed)?

_____
_____
_____

Chapter 12 You Can't Make It With Negative Peers

1) Are there negative people in my immediate circle that should be packed up and moved out of my space and territory for life?

_____
_____
_____

Chapter 13 Build Positive Energy Around Yourself

1) How can I be sure that everyone I have chosen to keep in my new immediate circle will make a positive impact on my success?

_____
_____
_____

2) What positive skills will each individual contribute to my success?

_____

_____

_____

Chapter 14 Build Credibility With Others Along The Way

1) Am I taking the right and appropriate measures to build credibility with others in my current industry?

_____

_____

_____

Chapter 15 Prepare For Change Before It Comes

1) What precautions am I taking in my life to prepare for any unexpected changes that may occur at any moment?

_____

_____

_____

Chapter 16 Let Go Of What You Can't Change

1) What are some of the things in my life that I cannot change and need to let go in order for me to become successful?

_____

_____

_____

Chapter 17 Plan Your Goals

1) What steps do I need to take in order to plan my goals effectively so that they come to life?

_____
_____
_____

Chapter 18 Set Real Life Goals

1) After planning my goals, what steps do I still need to take in order to make them come to life?

_____
_____
_____

Chapter 19 Clear The Clutter And Visualize Your Goals

1) What steps have I taken to clear the clutter from my mind that is blocking the perfect vision of my goals?

_____
_____
_____

Chapter 20 Act Today For A Better Tomorrow

1) If we don't act today, how can we look forward to a better tomorrow?

_____
_____
_____

Final Thoughts

I like to think of myself as a modern day "quoter" of my time. I love discovering a new quote and sharing it with my family, friends, and followers. When I come across a quote that I can relate to or is said so powerfully regardless of who said it, I add it to my mental Rolodex for safekeeping.

Over the years, I've come across so many different important quotes from so many entrepreneurs who have succeeded in life that stood out for me when I was either listening to them on TV or reading about them on their journeys. In this book, I wanted to share with you some of those quotes and I hope that made a difference in your day-to-day life, as they have done for me. One of the reasons I enjoy reading all types of books is because I learn from others that have been where I am in my life today and where I am still planning to go. I have read over 500 books of all genres since high school.

To this day, I am still a very consistent book reader. So when I come across quotes that make so much sense to me and can be related to the life I live or another's life, I hang on to them for dear life. Together these quotes of inspiration can make a difference in our lives regardless of what we are going through on any given day! I hope that my personal quotes have inspired you as well.

By sharing my real life experiences, I also hope that I was able to set the stage and be the advocate you needed me to be in order to make a difference in your life. I want to personally thank you for purchasing and reading my book. I look forward to sharing more of my books with you soon!

While there were many other successful individuals with awesome life quotes, I could not include them all. If the vision presents itself, in another one of my self-help titles, you will get to read more life quotes from other successful entrepreneurs around the world. If you enjoyed reading BYOLC, please leave a review on Amazon and sign my guest book on my website. Thanks ☺

References

Chapter 1 What Does Life Mean To You?
1. Merriam-Webster Online Dictionary. (2012). Life. Retrieved from http://www.merriam-webster.com/dictionary/life. (Found in this book on page 5)

Chapter 4 Know What Your Purpose Is In Life
1. Maxwell, J. C. (2010). *A Leader's Heart: 365 Day Devotional Journal*. Nashville, TN: Thomas Nelson. (Found in this book on page 15)

2. In an email conversation in Fall of 2010, the author of *The Skin I'm In* and *Begging For Change,* she advised that I focus on finishing one book. (Found in this book on page 16)

3. Wubbolding, R. E. (2000). *Reality Therapy for the 21st Century*. Philadelphia, PA: Brunner-Routledge. (Found in this book on page 17)

Chapter 5 Dare To Dream But Don't Strive For Another's Dream
1. Altman, J. (2002) *1,001 Dreams: An illustrated guide to dreams and their meanings*. San Francisco, CA: Chronicle Books. (Found in this book on page 19)

2. Dream Moods Inc. (2017). *What's in your dream?* Retrieved from http://www.dreammoods.com/commondreams/death-dreams.html. (Found in this book on page 19)

3. Gibson, T. (2011). *How to Get Out of Your Own Way*. New York: Grand Central Publishing. (Found in this book on page 20)

4. Garrett, S. (2002). *A Tap Water Girl in a Bottled Water World*. Alpharetta, GA: The Speaker Group, 15. (Found in this book on page 21)

5. Kardashian, K., Kardashian, K., & Kardashian, K. (2010). *Kardashian Konfidential.* New York, NY: Random House, 143. (Found in this book on page 22)

6. Baisden, M. (2012, June 27). Individual Broadcast. Miami, FL: HOT 105.1 FM. Michael Baisden quoted "Do not let anyone rob you of your dreams. Do something creative or you will never be happy." (Found in this book on page 22)

Chapter 6 Think Like A Leader To Become One

1. Maxwell, J. C. (2010). *A Leader's Heart: 365 Day Devotional Journal.* Nashville, TN: Thomas Nelson, 6. (Found in this book on page 26)

Chapter 7 Understand Failing Is Only The Beginning

1. Merriam-Webster Online Dictionary. (2012). Failing. Retrieved from http://www.merriam-webster.com/dictionary/failing. (Found in this book on page 29)

2. Merriam-Webster Online Dictionary. (2012). Failure. Retrieved from http://www.merriam-webster.com/dictionary/failure. (Found in this book on page 29)

3 Maxwell, J. C. (2000). *Failing Forward: Turning Mistakes Into Stepping Stones For Success.* Nashville, TN: Thomas Nelson, 27. (Found in this book on pages 29 and 30)

4. At Home with Tiny & T. I. (2012, February). Interview. *Sister 2 Sister,* 24 (2), 54–61. (Found in this book on page 31)

5. Steve Harvey: 8 Secrets to Make Millions. (2012, August). Interview. D. Millner (Interviewer/Writer). *EBONY Magazine* (The Black Wealth Issue), LXVII (10), 103–105. (Found in this book on page 32)

Chapter 8 Check Out Your Competition

1. Carter, S. (Jay Z). (2010). *Decoded.* New York, NY: Random House, 71. (Found in this book on pages 36 and 37)

2. Seals-Allers, K. (2009). *The Mocha Manual to Turning Your Passion to Profit.* New York, NY: Harpers-Collins, 167. (Found in this book on page 36)

3. Earvin "Magic" Johnson: Nothing But Net. (2012, July 23). Interview. M. Turner (West Coast Senior Writer/ Producer). *JET Magazine,* 121(15), 20–24. (Found in this book on page 37)

Chapter 9 Utilize Your Resources

1. Shakur, T. (2003). *Resurrection* [Motion Picture]. NStar Studios. (Found in this book on page 40)

2. Carter, S. (Jay Z). (2010). *Decoded.* New York, NY: Random House, 71. (Found in this book on page 40)

3. Kardashian, K., Kardashian, K., & Kardashian, K. (2010). *Kardashian Konfidential.* New York, NY: Random House, 214. (Found in this book on page 41)

4. Obama, B. (2006). *The Audacity of Hope: Thoughts on Reclaiming the American Dream.* New York, NY: Crown, 150. (Found in this book on page 41)

Chapter 10 Understand Others' Purpose In Your Life

1. Hall, A. (2011). Next runner up [Television series episode]. In O. Winfrey (Executive producer). The Oprah Winfrey Show. Chicago, IL: Harpo Productions. (Found in this book on page 44)

Chapter 12 You Can't Make It With Negative Peers

1. Merriam-Webster Online Dictionary. (2012). Negative. Retrieved from http://www.merriam-webster.com/dictionary/negative. (Found in this book on page 49)

2. DeGeneres, E. (2011). *Seriously, I'm Kidding.* New York, NY: Grand Central, 14. (Found in this book on page 50)

Chapter 13 Build Positive Energy Around Yourself
1. Merriam-Webster Online Dictionary. (2012). Energy. Retrieved from http://www.merriam-webster.com/dictionary/energy. (Found in this book on page 51)

2. Henson, T. P. (2011, November 2) Wendy Williams Show [Television show]. New York, NY: Talk WW Production. (Found in this book on page 52)

Chapter 14 Build Credibility With Others Along The Way
1. Kelley, K. (2010). *Oprah: A Biography.* New York, NY: Random House, 575. (Found in this book on page 55)

2. Monique: Staying True to Herself. (2010, April 5). Interview. M. Turner (West Coast Senior Writer/ Producer). *JET Magazine,* 117(13), 28–35. (Found in this book on page 56)

3. *Holy Bible: New Living Translation.* (2004). A Living Sacrifice to God (Romans 12:6–8). Carol Stream, IL: Tyndale House, 866. (Found in this book on page 57)

4. Harvey, S., & Millner, D. (2010). *Straight Talk, No Chaser: How to Find, Keep, and Understand a Man.* New York, NY: Amistad, 110. (Found in this book on page 58)

5. Run, R. (2008). *Words of Wisdom: Daily Affirmations of Faith from Run's House to Yours.* New York, NY: Harpers-Collins, 1. (Found twice in this book on page 59)

Chapter 15 Prepare For Change Before It Comes
1. Nelly. (2011). Interview. *Sister 2 Sister,* January. (Found in this book on page 61)

Chapter 16 Let Go Of What You Can't Change
1. Strawberry, S., & Beth LeFlore, L. (2011). *Strawberry Letter.* NY: Our World Books (an imprint of The Random House Publishing Group). (Found in this book on page 63)

2. Kelley, K. (2010). *Oprah: A Biography.* New York, NY: Random House, 545. (Found in this book on page 63)

3. Adelaja, S. (2009) *Money Won't Make You Rich.* Lake Mary, FL: Charisma House, 21. (Found in this book on page 68)

Chapter 17 Plan Your Goals

1. Fishman, S. (2005). *How New York's Shock Jockette Got Supersized: She Wants it Big. She Wants it Wendy.* Retrieved from http://nymag.com/print/?/nymetro/news/people/features/14790/index1.html. (Found in this book on page 69)

Chapter 18 Set Real Life Goals

1. Smith, I, (2008). *The 4 Day Diet.* New York, NY: ST. Martin's Press. (Found in this book on page 76)

2. Platinum Creative. (2011). *Full Sail Degree Guide Pamphlet: Your career goal* (Section 5). Winter Park, FL: Full Sail. (Found in this book on page 76)

3. In a tweet on February 28, 2011 at 6:00 pm Eastern Time, Joseph Simmons also known as Reverend Run, tweeted, "You will only have SIGNIFICANT success when you're border line obsessed with your goals." (Found in this book on page 78)

Chapter 19 Clear The Clutter And Visualize Your Goals

1. Sargent, A. C. (1999). *The Other Mind's Eye: The Gateway to the Hidden Treasures of Your Mind.* Malibu, CA: Success Design International. (Found in this book on pages 79 and 80)

2. Merriam-Webster Online Dictionary. (2012). Visualize. Retrieved from http://www.merriam-webster.com/dictionary/visualize. (Found in this book on page 80)

Chapter 20 Act Today For A Better Tomorrow

1. In a telephone conversation in Spring of 2011, the author of four New York Times Bestsellers at the time and founder of Jennings Solutions, Jason Jennings, he quoted that "Half of winning is being the last one standing." (Found in this book on page 86)

About The Author

Dr. Dionna Hancock-Johnson has published her first children's series, entitled *Where Did My Half-Brother Come From?*, which is designed to help children ages 4 to 8 embrace their half-siblings when they are introduced to their family through a difficult parenting situation or live outside of the home due to divorce or separation. Dr. Dionna has read her children's series at several childcare centers, elementary and middle schools in South Florida and Los Angeles. She is currently working on her next set of books and memoir due to be released soon.

Dr. Hancock-Johnson earned a Bachelor's of Arts from the University of Oregon in Psychology and Sociology, a Master's of Science from Iowa State University in Human Development and Family Studies with a specialization in Family Studies, and a Doctorate of Education (EdD) in Counseling Psychology with a concentration in Counselor Education and Supervision. She has also gained additional certification as a Life Strategies Coach (LSC) in Rancho Santa Margarita, CA. Dr. Hancock-Johnson has been mentioned in *The Monitor, Miami Today,* and *Coffee News* (Palmetto Bay Edition). Most recently, she did an interview with Miami's Hot 105.1 FM Radio Station with Rodney Baltimore.

Dr. Hancock-Johnson is the founder of Energetic Life Coaching (ELC), LLC, the Hancock-Johnson Publishing Company, the Hancock-Johnson Empire, and Hancock-Johnson Corporation.

Dr. Hancock-Johnson offers several Life Coaching Programs for individuals from all walks of life. Her passion is working with young women and men to help them find their purpose in life. Dr. Hancock-Johnson is also a motivational speaker and has presented at meet & greets, book signings, national conferences, graduations, private organizations, and small businesses, as well to general audiences, speaking on topics related to blended families, motivation, molestation, abuse, building positive energy, and overcoming difficult life situations.

Dr. Hancock-Johnson is married to Cephus R. Johnson, and together they have a son named Cephus De'Moni Johnson, also known as Cj, and a daughter named Ce'Onna Meilani Johnson, also known as Ce'Onna Meilani. Together they enjoy trying new family activities and hanging with their Maltipoo, Skippy.

To contact Dr. Dionna Hancock-Johnson for personal life coaching services or questions, visit http://www.drdionna.com and http://www.energeticlifecoaching.com.

If you are interested in booking Dr. Dionna as a speaker for one of your events, company appreciation days, graduation address ceremonies, or other booking events, contact her personal assistant at drdionnasassistant@gmail.com.

To follow Dr. Dionna for inspiration, check her out on Facebook at https://facebook.com/drdionnalifecoach, Instagram at https://www.instagram.com/drdionnalifecoach, and Twitter at http://www.twitter.com/DionnaLifeCoach.

About The Photographer, Cover Designer, And Editors

Scott Hebert of Studio 360 Productions, provided Dr. Dionna's headshot on the back cover. Scott, a well-known celebrity photographer, producer, videographer, and director, resides in Los Angeles, CA. If you want to know more about him or book him for your next project, he can be reached at info@scotthebert.com. To follow Scott Hebert's work, check out http://scotthebert.com and on social media @travelwithscott.

Donavan Day, better known in Dionna's Children's Series as Hassani Kwess, provided the basic graphics to the original BYOLC cover. Donavan is an up-and-coming independent music artist who has talent in producing, singing, rapping, and drawing/illustration. If you want to know more about him or to book him for you next book or music project, he can be reached at hygherpower@gmail.com. To follow Hassani Kwess work, you can check him out on social media @hassanikwess.

John and Sue Morris of Editide provided valuable editorial and design services. Editide can be reached at info@editide.us and http://www.editide.us. The couple offers comprehensive word and graphic services to clients on six continents, specializing in academic and nonfiction dissertations, articles, books, and memoirs.

Current And Future Products From Dr. Dionna Hancock-Johnson

Children's Books
Half-Brother/Step-Brother Series
Where Did My Half-Brother Come From? (Half-Brother Series 1)

Half-Sister/Step-Sister Series
Where Did My Half-Sister Come From? (Half-Sister Series 1)

Young Adult/Teen Books
I Am Just Anotha DC Girl Living In A Different World

Self-Help Books
Be Your Own Life Coach: How to Life Coach Yourself into What You Want

Be Your Own Life Coach: How to Life Quote Yourself into What You Want

The Beginner's Guide to Getting Your Kids into the Entertainment Business

The Beginner's Guide to Protecting Your Kids in the Entertainment Business

Self-Help eBooks
How to Redefine You after a Break-Up, Divorce or Family Separation: 10 Ways to Redefine Yourself into What You Want

Self-Help Courses
16 Tips to Market Your Business Without the Internet: Beginners Course

Self-Help Audio CD
Be Your Own Life Coach: How to Life Coach Yourself into What You Want Within the Comfort of Your Own Home

Autobiography
From Devastation to Doctorate: How I Went from Molestation to Magnificent

www.ingramcontent.com/pod-product-compliance
Lightning Source LLC
Chambersburg PA
CBHW050438010526
44118CB00013B/1582